"Finally, a clear, exegetical, pacovenant theology! The autho.book promises to be a valuable resource for Sunday school classes, discipleship groups, and personal study. It is a fresh and thoroughly biblical account of an all-important subject. Read it, and then read it again. I warmly commend this book!"

> **Dr. Jon D. Payne,** *Pastor of Grace Presbyterian Church (PCA) in Douglasville, GA, and author of* In the Splendor of Holiness: Rediscovering the Beauty of Reformed Worship for the 21st Century

"Brown and Keele have produced an introduction to covenant theology (and therefore biblical theology) that has several distinctive features: First, it is eminently readable and clear; second, it is compellingly biblical in its reasoning and conclusions, constantly displaying the biblical texts in which the various covenants are narrated; and third, it frequently cites covenant theologians and Reformed confessions from the past, locating itself solidly in the mainstream of that tradition. For over twenty-five years, my students have asked for a book such as this, a book that surveys in lucid fashion the various biblical covenants in their chronological order, demonstrating both their intrinsic unity as part of God's plan to rescue Adam's race in Christ and their particular distinctive features as well."

> **T. David Gordon,** *Professor of New Testament and Greek, Grove City College*

"Michael Brown and Zach Keele have done the admirable job of producing a survey of covenant theology that is Reformed, engaging, and accessible. Each chapter seamlessly weaves lines of biblical and theological argument, plainly demonstrates the practical importance of the covenants of God with his people, and helpfully concludes with questions suitable for group discussion or personal reflection. While not every reader will agree with every argument of *Sacred Bond*, this work merits a place in the front rank of a growing literature designed to acquaint Reformed Christians with the riches of their heritage. "Covenant theology," C.H. Spurgeon once said, "glorifies God alone." It "puts man aside, and makes him a debtor and receiver . . . plung[ing] him into the sea of infinite grace and unmerited favor." Let *Sacred Bond* show you how it is that covenant theology "glorifies God alone," so that you may better think and live to the glory of God."

> **Dr. Guy Waters,** *Associate Professor of New Testament, Reformed Theological Seminary, Jackson, MS City College*

*Michael G. Brown
and Zach Keele*

Sacred Bond

Covenant Theology Explored

Reformed Fellowship, Inc.
3500 Danube Drive SW
Grandville MI 49418

Sacred Bond

© 2012 by Michael G. Brown and Zach Keele
All rights reserved.

Scripture quotations are from The Holy Bible, English Standard Version® (ESV®), copyright © 2001 by Crossway, a publishing ministry of Good News Publishers. Used by permission. All rights reserved.

Reformed Fellowship, Inc. is a religious and strictly nonprofit organization composed of a group of Christian believers who hold to the biblical Reformed faith. Our purpose is to advocate and propagate this faith, to nurture those who seek to live in obedience to it, to give sharpened expression to it, to stimulate the doctrinal sensitivities of those who profess it, to promote the spiritual welfare and purity of the Reformed churches, and to encourage Christian action.

Requests for permission to quote from this book should be directed to:

Reformed Fellowship, Inc.
3500 Danube Dr. SW
Grandville, MI 49418
(877) 532-8510
president@reformedfellowship.net
www.reformedfellowship.net

Book design by Jeff Steenholdt.

Printed in the United States of America

ISBN 978-1-935369-04-2

Dedicated
to
the Pilgrim-Saints
at
Christ United Reformed Church
&
Escondido Orthodox Presbyterian Church

Contents

Foreword **8**

Introduction: What Is Covenant Theology, and Why Should I Care? **10**

Grace before Time: The Covenant of Redemption **23**

Failure in Paradise: The Covenant of Works **41**

I Will Be Your God: The Covenant of Grace **57**

Promise in the Clouds: The Common Grace Covenant **73**

I Will Give to You: The Abrahamic Covenant **85**

Don't Spare the Rod: The Mosaic Covenant **101**

The King Who Did: The Davidic Covenant **121**

Dawn of the New Creation: The New Covenant **135**

Glossary of Terms **153**

Scripture Index **156**

Name Index **164**

Foreword

We live in a world of broken promises. Just pick up the newspaper, listen to conversations among friends and spouses, or think of your own experience of being let down—even letting others down. In sharp contrast, the triune God has never made a promise he failed to keep. Throughout biblical history, he compares his covenant people to a bride whom he has lavished with his gifts. Although she often uses her beauty to attract other lovers and squanders her wealth on adulterous affairs, the Lord keeps his promise. "If we remain faithless, he remains faithful, for he cannot deny himself" (2 Tim. 2:13). It's not a contract, but a covenant, and the kind of covenant that is secured on God's side, by his faithfulness, at the greatest personal cost.

Unpacking this major theme from Genesis to Revelation is the exciting opportunity before you with this book. Besides filling you with wonder again at the God of all grace, this book will be of tremendous value in providing the right distinctions and categories for interpreting Scripture.

What's the relationship between the Old and New Testaments? Some parts of the Bible make it sound as if everything depends on our faithfulness, while others make it seem as if God's faithfulness is the only ground of the relationship. Is there a way of resolving this apparent contradiction? Are all of God's promises fulfilled in Christ, or are some yet to be fulfilled in a restored nation of Israel? How do the New Testament apostles interpret the Old Testament prophecies?

These are not just academic questions but also lie at the heart of our reading, hearing, and living out of the biblical story.

Besides giving you a better map of the biblical terrain, this book provides the framework for the most important questions in the Christian life.

What's the nature of our relationship with God? How does it determine our relationship to the visible church, our family, and our social and cultural engagement? What is our calling as God's image-bearers and as those who belong to his kingdom? How do preaching, baptism, and the Lord's Supper fit in with our daily discipleship? These and many other important questions are addressed here in a down-to-earth, richly scriptural, and pastoral way.

Michael Brown and Zach Keele are pastor-scholars who not only study these issues closely but also have had the opportunity to apply the Bible's covenant theology to the lives of believers, week in and week out. Sitting under their ministry, my family and I can give first-hand testimony to their remarkable gifts. I am deeply impressed not only with their wisdom and insight but also with their ability to explain the Bible and its covenants with remarkable clarity and accessibility.

So read, mark, learn, and inwardly digest this wonderful guide. In doing so, you will be much better equipped to know what you believe and why you believe it.

Michael Horton
Professor of Theology and Apologetics
Westminster Seminary California

Introduction:
WHAT IS COVENANT THEOLOGY, AND WHY SHOULD I CARE?

So what is a covenant? Covenant is not a word we use in our everyday lives. If you are an attorney, you may use it occasionally. But outside of certain legal uses, we don't come across this word very often. It rings with a foreign and archaic tone, as if you are hearing *Taming of the Shrew* read with a sharp British accent.

Yet in the church, the word *covenant* is often batted around like a tennis ball between the rackets of love and hate. Some use it in a derogatory manner, others to make themselves seem smarter than they are. Many hear it only to roll their eyes, not quite knowing what it means. Still others put it in every other sentence that escapes from their mouths. Covenant can be one of those words that Christians hear and use, but everyone is afraid to ask the definition. Inevitably, this has led to an underappreciation of the term and, in some cases, misunderstanding and confusion.

Anyone who has read the Bible, however, knows that the word *covenant* appears frequently on its pages. The book of Genesis is primarily about God's covenant with Abraham and his descendants, which was built on God's first gospel promise to Adam and Eve in Genesis 3:15. And the book of Exodus records God's covenant with the nation Israel. All the way through the Old Testament, in its historical books, psalms, and prophetical books, these two covenants are referred to over and over again. When we come to the New Testament, we are told of Jesus instituting a new covenant, the same covenant of which the prophet Jeremiah foretold (Jer. 31:31–34).

Moreover, the apostle Paul discusses in detail the differences between God's covenant with Abraham and his covenant with the nation Israel (Gal. 3–4), as well as the difference between the latter and the new covenant (2 Cor. 3). And we haven't even mentioned the fact that God also made important covenants with Noah and David! It is safe to say, therefore, that covenant is a vital aspect of Scripture. In fact, it is more accurate to state that covenant is the very fabric of Scripture. It is God's chosen framework for the Bible.

But in order to understand and appreciate what a covenant is in its more technical use in theology, it is helpful to examine it at a more basic level. We may not realize it, but the essential stuff of a covenant is almost an everyday reality for us. So what is a covenant? *A covenant is a formal agreement that creates a relationship with legal aspects.* By *relationship*, we do not mean merely those relationships of husband-wife, or government-citizen—though these are included—but also the relationship of giving your word to do something. If you tell your neighbors that you will feed their dogs while they are on vacation, this is a commitment or agreement. You have a relationship with your neighbor just by being her neighbor, but giving your word that you will feed the dogs is a commitment, a covenant of sorts. A covenant can be a commitment, promise, or oath. In fact, in the Bible, promise and oath are often used as synonyms for covenant.

So a covenant can be an agreement of just about any sort. Yet it is also legal. Now, a legal relationship does not only apply to the court system. Courts, laws, judges, and police are part of what it means to be legal. Yet legality at a more basic level means there are duties with consequences; punishments or sanctions are involved. These consequences can be more formal, such as getting fined by the law, or they can be less formal, such as discipline by a parent. The consequences of shame, disfavor, or wrath for not keeping one's promise at times can be more powerful than the punishments of courts.

Too often, we put legality in opposition to intimate relationships. We tend to think there is nothing legal about the parent-child relationship, as if it were only about love and mercy. But this is hardly the case. The love and intimacy of the parent-child relationship does not make it void of legality. In fact, it may increase its legal character. As Hebrews points out, the father who does not discipline his children does not love them (12:7–8). Children by birth are obligated to their parents and vice versa. If children don't do their chores, there are consequences. If parents don't care for their kids, there are consequences. True, the vast majority of the consequences are not dealt with in a court of law, but the consequences of anger from a loved one, losing trust, and being denied privileges still sting. In an honor-and-shame society, as was the culture of ancient Israel, to be shamed by a parent could be worse than death. The consequence may be having one's reputation hurt or getting laughed at, but it is still a consequence, and this gives it a legal character. Thus, there is no tension between the fact that a covenant is a relationship—even one with loving intimacy—and the fact that a covenant is legal and has legal consequences. An ideal example of this is marriage, which the Lord calls a covenant (Mal. 2:14). The intimacy between a man and woman in wedlock is not hindered by the legality of marriage; instead, the legal vows intensify the intimacy.

The basic building blocks of covenant, therefore, are found every time one promises to do something for someone else with the implied positive and negative consequences determined by the cultural and relational context. The promise creates a relationship. It is a commitment with implied sanctions, like in those old western films when the cowboy says, "A man's word is law around here." Speaking creates commitments; our words bind us to actions and to other people. Rudimentary morality tells us that our actions should fit our words, for them to be otherwise is shameful and wrong. Our Lord pointed to this in the Sermon on the Mount when he said our yes should be yes and our no, no (Matt. 5:37). We have all experienced the crush of shame when we failed to keep our word, and a friend said, "I can't believe you broke your promise."

Once one grasps that the principal elements of covenant permeate our everyday existence, it becomes much easier to understand the biblical covenants, for a covenant in its fuller sense is merely a formalization of these everyday commitments. If a husband tells his wife he will pick up the dry cleaning on his way home from work, he has given his word to her. If he forgets, the consequence is that his wife will be upset. Yet if it is of the utmost importance that he doesn't forget the dry cleaning, the wife will stop her forgetful man and make him promise not to forget. She may even add explicit and more serious consequences: he will have to go back and get it, or no golfing on the weekend. The commitment to get the dry cleaning gets formalized with more explicit promises and consequences.

An amusing example of this is found in Disney's original *Robin Hood* cartoon, when the little boy has to recover his arrow after shooting it over the wall into Prince John's castle. He and his friends are afraid the turtle Toby will tattle on them, so they make him take an oath, saying, "Put your hand on your heart and cross your eyes and say: 'Spiders, snakes, and a lizard's head; if I tattletale, I'll die till I'm dead.'" The oath or covenant makes more serious that Toby has to keep his word not to tell; the oath formalizes the agreement. As kids, we may remember taking a similar oath with our friends: "Cross your heart, hope to die, stick a needle in my eye." The exaggerated consequence of dying fits a child's clear-cut view of life.

These promissory commitments, then, go through greater formalization and standardization in all parts of society. Virtually every contract is a covenant, from mortgages to car loans to peace treaties. They are formalized commitments or agreements between parties that state duties and consequences down to the finest detail made applicable for all people. Different names are given to such contracts according to the specific occasion or use, but, at the core, they are covenants.

Covenants in the Ancient World

The use of covenants in the ancient world was essentially the same. They were commitments that created a relationship with sanctions. Of course, Israel belonged to an ancient and foreign culture, and so the form and function of their covenants varied from ours. In an honor-and-shame society, and one where family was a key part of the legal structure, a person's word carried considerable weight. Moreover, the ancient Near East was not a modern or scientific society. Their rules for evidence differed from those in our culture. Our society is somewhat less dependent on a person's word. We are able to test a person's word with evidence: recordings, fingerprints, and DNA tests. Not so in the ancient world. Without witnesses, there was no sure way to test one's word externally. Also, deism and atheism did not exist in the ancient world. The Israelites and all their neighbors believed that their respective deities were actively involved in human life and history. The gods directed the events of life and one's well-being. And the gods would adjudicate wrongs committed.

Hence, covenants involved oaths whereby one swore by a god to do something or to tell the truth, and if not, then the god would judge the person. If a person swore that he was telling the truth, and the next day a lion ate him, an ancient would assume he had lied, and the god had judged him. The belief that the gods would punish them made them take care with their oaths. Since oaths in ancient society were commonly understood and usually expected to appear in a particular form, the Bible often abbreviates the oaths it describes. The short form of an oath is, "As the Lord lives, I will . . ." One swore by something greater than oneself, something more certain and firm, and nothing is greater than the life of the Lord. The full form, which is often dropped, includes the sanction, "Let me be cursed," typically by death. The full form includes a cursing of oneself, not that different from Toby's oath in *Robin Hood*. This self-curse is called *self-maledictory*. The person taking the oath is asking God to curse him if he breaks his oath.

Since taking an oath was such a solemn act, it was often accompanied by rites or ceremonies, typically in a temple or in the presence of a god. These ceremonies acted out in symbolic fashion the nature of the relationship and the consequences of breaking one's commitment. In a similar fashion, today's marriage ceremonies act out the character of the relationship being made. The vows are promises with implied sanctions if broken. The rings are signs of the relationship and express the couple's love for one another. In fact, if you have ever purchased a house, then you know the signing of escrow papers is almost a ceremony; the piles of paper, the hundreds of signatures and large figures are quite effective to impress on you that this is a serious commitment and contract.

In Israel's day, however, these ceremonies tended to be far more vivid and gruesome, at least by our standards. Because the sanction for not keeping one's covenant oath was the curse of death, the people making a covenant would kill animals as a symbol of their death. This even comes across in the Hebrew idiom for making a covenant, which is literally "to cut a covenant." The cutting referred to the ceremony of killing and cutting animals in half. As one scholar states in reference to this cutting, "This gesture seems to have become so widespread and common that it may have turned into a kind of prevalent supplement to a covenant ceremony."[1]

There is more to the covenant ceremonies than just the cutting of animals. Clearly, the verbal oath-taking of the parties was the central part. Witnesses, either personal or inanimate, often had a part. Also, one or both parties might make various gestures. These gestures could be directed at each other or to the god(s). Such gestures, like the giving of the ring in a marriage ceremony, dramatized the love, loyalty, and commitment of the relationship. A common gesture was a shared meal between the parties who made the covenant. Often, they ate the animals cut in the covenant ceremony. Such a meal was reflective of their committed relationship. It is necessary to remember that even though these covenant ceremonies had numerous common elements, they were still flexible. Parts could be added, subtracted, or fashioned to fit the specific relationship and occasion. We should not impute a false rigidity to the ceremonies, for the form and ceremony of the covenant matched the relationship.

So, ancient covenants were formal relationships or agreements bound with oaths. In the sphere of family, marriage and adoption were considered covenants. In the public sphere, covenants included treaties between nations (Joshua and the Gibeonites in Josh. 9; Israel with Assyria in Hos. 12:1), laws and agreements between kings and their people (King Zedekiah in Jer. 34:8–18), contracts in business (Abraham and Abimelech in Gen. 21:22–30), commitments between friends (Jonathan and David in 1 Sam. 20:16), and agreements between masters and servants (Abner with David in 2 Sam. 3:12; Laban and Jacob in Gen. 31:44). We could give more examples, but this gives a good spectrum, illustrating how a covenant must be flexible for the relationship. Both marriage and international treaties are covenants;

---

1. Menahem Haran, "The *Berit* 'Covenant': Its Nature and Ceremonial Background," in *Tehillah le-Moshe: Biblical and Judaic Studies in Honor of Moshe Greenberg* (ed. Mordecai Cogan, Barry L. Eichler and Jeffrey H. Tigay; Winona Lake: Eisenbrauns, 1997), 203–219.

however, the forms of these covenants differ. Likewise in the Bible, it is imperative to pay attention to the form of a particular covenant to grasp its nature.

The familial and secular use of covenants in the ancient Near East provides the necessary background for us to understand the religious covenants of the Bible. For as God makes covenants with his people, he does so in ways they understand. God accommodated to what was normal for Abraham, Moses, and the Israelites. If God made a covenant with us today, he would use the common legal and personal agreements that our society uses. This does not mean that the spiritual covenants are exhausted in their secular counterparts, but it does mean that our understanding of the biblical covenants begins with an understanding of the common ancient covenants. This is how it was for the Hebrews, and so it is for us. As we shall see, the biblical covenants far surpass any common covenant of human society. In fact, God's covenants pull together aspects from marriage, adoption, treaties, friendship, kingdom, and lord/servant.

Furthermore, the Lord's accommodation to use ancient covenants does not mean these are the original pattern. Reformed theologians have rightly confessed that the original pattern for God's covenant with his people is the perfect communion found in the Trinity. The Reformed theologian Louis Berkhof (1873–1957) said it well:

> Covenants among men had been made long before God established His covenant with Noah and with Abraham, and this prepared men to understand the significance of a covenant in a world divided by sin, and helped them to understand the divine revelation, when it presented man's relation to God as a covenant relation. This does not mean, however, that the covenant idea originated with man and was then borrowed by God as an appropriate form for the description of the mutual relationship between Himself and man. Quite the opposite is true; the archetype of all covenant life is found in the Trinitarian being of God, and what is seen among men is but a faint copy of this.[2]

---

2. *Systematic Theology*, 263.

Covenant life is reflected in human society because it flows from God's Trinitarian existence. The Father, Son, and Holy Spirit live in unceasing devotion and commitment to each other. As Michael Horton writes, God reached "outward beyond the Godhead to create a community of creatures, serving as a giant analogy of the Godhead's relationship."[3] As creatures made in the image of God, we should be eager to grasp the significance of the ancient covenants in order to appreciate and understand more fully our relationship with our God and Savior. We study the ancient parallels, not as an end in and of themselves, but as the necessary avenue to know and love our Lord with greater fervor. God in his sovereign wisdom appointed such covenants as a means to show his love to us. We should gratefully use them as background to God's Word.

How Should We Then Define a Covenant?

The preceding discussion demonstrates that a more general definition is necessary. The wide use of covenant with specific applications to definite relationships demands flexibility. Therefore, *a covenant is a solemn agreement with oaths and/or promises, which imply certain sanctions or legality.* Covenants have a certain formality to them so that they are by definition more than a casual promise. There must be at least two parties. These parties can be equals (marriage) or unequals (superior to inferior). And the nature of the relationship can vary. They can be intimate or impersonal. The sanctions can be minor or drastic. The classic definition of covenant as a "mutual agreement between two parties" is adequate, provided it is not applied too literally, for covenants are not limited to two parties. Moreover, covenants do not have to be mutual. Mutual suggests both parties willingly agree to the covenant relationship. Yet a superior can impose a covenant on an inferior where the inferior party has no real choice.

Our concern, however, is with the biblical covenants, and so a definition for biblical covenants is helpful. There are three key points.
- The covenants we are concerned with in Scripture are God's covenants with his people or mankind in general.
- God is the author and initiator of them.

---

3. Michael Horton, *God of Promise* (Grand Rapids: Baker, 2006), 10.

- They are divine commitments bound by oath—God's promises or oaths to humans with seals and/or signs.

Specifying beyond this will not serve us well. To add adjectives such as "gracious" or "redemptive" to all covenants in Scripture will inevitably prejudice one's analysis of different covenants and their administrations. All of God's dealings with humanity are accommodations, but they are not always gracious; that is, they do not always give undeserved favor to one who deserves judgment. In fact, since covenants are by definition legal, *all* divine covenants are legal, though not all are gracious. Precise definitions for distinct covenants and their respective administrations are necessary. Yet over-precision on the basic definition will only hinder accuracy in the specific. Therefore, definitions for the various covenants will follow in their respective chapters.

In addition to a definition, it is worth mentioning the role that divine covenants play in Scripture. God's purpose in history is to govern his kingdom of creation and bring forth his holy kingdom. His covenants, therefore, are the way that God administers his kingdom. As God brings forth his redemptive kingdom from Genesis 3:15, he administers his kingdom through the covenant of grace and its different administrations. The Mosaic covenant is the constitution of the Israelite theocracy. The new covenant is the constitution for the church, the kingdom of heaven on earth. God's kingdom people are called the covenant community and citizens of heaven. God's covenants embody that relationship: what God has done for us, as well as our obligations to him. Hence, covenant is not a means to an end, but it is the end itself—the communion between God and his people.

Finally, it is helpful to consider some of the synonyms for covenant used in Scripture, or the various ways to which a covenant can be referred. Since a covenant is an oath-bound relationship, it is to be expected that this relationship can be identified in all sorts of ways. To use marriage as an example, we rarely use the word *covenant* to describe the relationship; instead, there are several words and metaphorical images for marriage, all or most of which connote the idea of covenant. Here is a list of the primary synonyms for covenant in Scripture, most of which are parts of the covenant relationship or ceremony that point to the whole.

Oath: It is to be expected that the most common synonym for covenant is oath. Since the relationship is embodied in the oath or promise of the parties to each other, the covenant relationship is regularly referred to by the oath. God's relationship to Abraham is explicitly called a covenant over and over. For example, Exodus 2:24 says, "God remembered his covenant with Abraham, with Isaac, and with Jacob." This same relationship is spoken by God's swearing an oath, so we read in Exodus 6:8, "I will bring you into the land that I swore to give to Abraham, to Isaac, and to Jacob. I will give it to you for a possession. I am the LORD." Likewise, God said to Isaac, "I will establish the oath that I swore to Abraham your father" (Gen. 26:3). This language, then, is found throughout the Old Testament and in the New Testament, especially in the book of Hebrews.

Promise: Since oaths have a promissory character, promise is also used as a synonym for covenant. Thus, in Galatians 3, Paul refers to the Abrahamic covenant merely as the promise.

Obligation: Covenant relationships contain obligations—often written—from one party to the other and vice versa. The mention of obligations can denote the whole covenant. Hence, depending on context, numerous words for obligations or stipulations are used to refer to the covenant: law(s), commandment(s), testimony, judgment(s), statute(s), and word(s). Think about how Paul regularly refers to the Sinai covenant merely as "the law," by its obligations.

Signs: The signs or symbols of covenant relationships are also used for the whole. As the wedding ring symbolizes the marriage, so also signs like circumcision and the Lord's Supper picture the whole. The Lord Jesus said of the cup in the Lord's Supper, "This cup is the new covenant."

Covenant formula: Another way to refer to a covenant is by a certain formula or summary statements, such as the sentence in Scripture called the covenant formula. The covenant formula is "I will be your God and you will by my people," and variations of it. This formula encapsulates the covenant relationship. Yet the foundational form is "I will be _____ to you and you will be _____ to me." The blanks can be filled with husband/wife, father/son, and Lord/servant. It is also often found in halves: "I will be . . ." or "you will be . . ." This formula permeates the Old Testament, and it finds a crowning position at the end of Scripture, when God says of his people in the New Jerusalem, "Behold, the dwelling place of God is with man. He will dwell with them, and they will be his people, and God himself will be with them as their God" (Rev. 21:3).

One final way a covenant can be referred to or identified is through covenantal terminology or ritual action. Hebrew words like *peace, love, steadfast love,* and *curse* are common covenant language. (These Hebrew words can be translated in varying ways in different English translations, so caution is required in dealing with the English.) This does not mean these words are technical terms *per se*, but they have a common use in covenants, so they regularly reflect a covenant relationship/context. An example of this is found in Deuteronomy 20:10, where before battle Israel offered "terms of peace" to certain cities (literally—"call to it for peace"). Here, "peace" is used as a synonym for "treaty" or "covenant." Likewise, certain ritual actions can demonstrate a covenant in this context: eating a meal, giving a blessing, or cutting animals.

From this introduction, it should become evident why covenant is vital to the Christian life. Covenant is our relationship with God and his with us. The curse we deserve for sin, how Christ saved us, how we please God, our prayer life, our blessed hope—all of these things are played out on the stage of covenant. The gospel message falters without its covenantal foundation. Our assurance of salvation is neutered without it. That is why the Reformed scholastic Francis Turretin (1623–87) stated this about the importance of covenant:

> Since [covenant] is of the greatest importance in theology (being as it were the center and bond of all religion, consisting in the communion of God with man and embracing in its compass all the benefits of God towards man and his duties towards God), our highest interest lies in rightly knowing and observing it. Hence the discussion of it demands peculiar accuracy (*akribeian*), that the truth may be confirmed against the errors by which Satan has endeavored in almost every age to obscure and corrupt this saving doctrine.[4]

---

4. Francis Turretin, *Institutes of Elenctic Theology*, ed. James T. Dennison (New Jersey: P&R, 1994), 2:169.

To study the covenants of Scripture is to learn about the great and majestic God we serve and behold his splendid grace and mercy to us in Jesus Christ. This introduction should also help us understand that *covenant theology* is not an abstract system imposed on the Bible, but the very structure and framework that naturally arises from Scripture itself as the drama of redemptive history unfolds from Genesis to Revelation. Covenant theology is the Bible's prescribed method of helping us interpret the Scriptures properly. Covenant theology helps us to deepen our understanding of God's salvation of and communion with his people through the person and work of Christ. It is God's way of giving us the big picture of his plan of redemption and showing us that his Word, from beginning to end, is consistent and not contradictory.

How to Use This Book

The following chapters explain eight significant covenants in Scripture: the covenant of redemption, the covenant of works, the covenant of grace, the Noahic covenant, the Abrahamic covenant, the Mosaic covenant, the Davidic covenant, and the new covenant. Each chapter has four parts. The first part gives a brief theological description of the particular covenant being discussed and provides a simple, one-sentence summary of the featured covenant.

The second part of each chapter deals with the biblical evidence for that covenant, answering the question, "What does the Bible teach?" It is one thing to give a theological definition of a doctrine, but it is another thing to show why that definition is biblical. Each chapter will aim to do just this, moving from the Old Testament to the New Testament.

The third part of each chapter considers briefly how that particular covenant is stated by the Reformed confessions and various Reformed theologians in history. We believe this is helpful to familiarize the reader with the way in which covenant theology has been expressed historically in the Reformed tradition. While the Reformers of the sixteenth and seventeenth centuries did not invent covenant theology but built on foundations already laid in the early church fathers and medieval periods in order to defend Protestant doctrine, it is nevertheless true that covenant theology *is* Reformed theology.

The fourth part of each chapter is intended to show why the specific doctrine is valuable for the Christian life. As we hope to make clear, covenant theology is not an intangible theory of abstract reasoning. Rather, it is the Bible's own structure that provides us with an immensely practical, concrete body of belief. This concludes with several questions for further reflection by the reader.

As pastors, we pray that you find this book helpful to your understanding of the person and work of Christ and the message of the gospel as it unfolds in redemptive history. We wrote this book because we have often found ourselves at a loss when asked by congregants for a good *introductory* resource on covenant theology. Although there are many excellent books on the subject, most, in our opinion, are not designed for the uninitiated layperson. Given the importance of covenant theology for the Christian life, we believe a book that provides a simple and clear explanation of each of the major covenants of Scripture is needed in the church today. This book is intended to be a means to that end, although it is in no way the final word on the vast subject of covenant theology. Rather, it is an introductory volume designed to give readers a basic grasp of this essential subject matter and encourage them to pursue further study. May the Lord bless you as you pursue a deeper knowledge of his plan of salvation as it is administered in his covenants!

1

Grace Before Time:
THE COVENANT OF REDEMPTION

We begin our survey of covenant theology with a consideration of that covenant from which all other biblical covenants flow, namely, the covenant of redemption. The covenant of redemption is essentially God's blueprint for our salvation. Just as a house, ship, or other structure begins with a plan of meticulous engineering and technical design, so also did our redemption originate on the drafting table of God. Before the creation of the world, a plan was already in place to send the Son as the second Adam to remedy the disastrous results of the first Adam's failure to fulfill the covenant of works in the garden of Eden and bring humankind to glory. The covenant of redemption was not a "plan B" to fix the mess Adam made, but the original blueprint for the work of Christ and the plan of redemption.

To put it another way, the covenant of redemption is like the original composition of a classical music masterpiece. Before anyone enjoyed the stunning concertos of *The Four Seasons,* Antonio Vivaldi composed the sounds in 1723 that would later become a timeless piece of art enjoyed for centuries. In similar fashion, God composed his masterpiece of redemption long before any human enjoyed its benefits. As we will see in this chapter, however, God's plan for our salvation was not only a *concept* but also an actual *covenant* between the persons of the Trinity.

What Is the Covenant of Redemption?

The covenant of redemption is the first of three overarching covenants in redemptive history, namely, *the covenant of redemption, the covenant of works,* and *the covenant of grace.* There are, of course, more covenants in Scripture, such as the Abrahamic covenant, the Mosaic covenant, and so on. As we will learn in the subsequent chapters of this book, however, these are subsets of the three overarching covenants. The first overarching covenant is the covenant of redemption. Sometimes referred to by its Latin title, *pactum salutis,* the covenant of redemption is the origin and firm foundation of the covenant of grace. Without it, there would be no election, no incarnation of the Son, no cross, no resurrection, and no promise of heaven. In short, there would be no salvation of sinners.

The covenant of redemption is unique for at least two other reasons. *First, it was made between the persons of the Trinity, and not, as in most biblical covenants, between God and humans.* The covenant of redemption is a pact between the Father, the Son, and the Holy Spirit with the purpose of redeeming God's elect. The Father gave to the Son those whom he chose to save and required him to accomplish their salvation though his obedient life and atoning death as the second Adam. He also promised the Son a reward on the completion of his work. The Son accepted the Father's gift, agreed to the conditions of this covenant, and submitted himself to the Father's will. The Holy Spirit promised to apply the benefits earned by the Son to the elect and unite them with the Son forever. Thus, we say the covenant of redemption is an *intratrinitarian* covenant between the Father, Son, and Holy Spirit.

Second, the covenant of redemption is unique because it was established before time. All other biblical covenants were made *in* time and history. The covenant of redemption, however, was made in eternity, before the foundation of the world and all things temporal. Thus, we say that it is a *pretemporal* covenant.

Therefore, behind all of God's covenanting with Adam, Noah, Abraham, Israel, David, and his elect, stands the covenant of redemption. Planned from eternity by the members of the Godhead, the covenant of redemption is the basis and driving purpose of all redemptive history. We give a summary definition of the covenant of redemption as *the covenant established in eternity between the Father, who gives the Son to be the Redeemer of the elect and requires of him the conditions for their redemption; and the Son, who voluntarily agrees to fulfill these conditions; and the Spirit, who voluntarily applies the work of the Son to the elect.*

What Does the Bible Teach?

We should not be alarmed that the Bible never mentions the phrase, "covenant of redemption." The Bible teaches many key doctrines without ever using the same terminology that theologians have coined for those doctrines. For example, Scripture teaches the doctrine of the Trinity, yet never uses the word *Trinity*. Nevertheless, we can still use the word *Trinity* to refer more easily to the teaching of Scripture that God is one in essence yet three in person. The doctrine of the covenant of redemption is no different. Although the exact phrase does not appear in the Bible, the doctrine itself does. This becomes evident as the drama of redemptive history unfolds. God's promise to send a Savior, first verbalized in Genesis 3:15, is progressively revealed in the Old Testament until it comes to fulfillment in the person and work of Christ. In the bright light of the New Testament, we see clearly that the relationship between the Father and the Son is *covenantal* in nature, involving a promised reward to the Son for his obedience to prescribed conditions. We now turn to a few of the many passages in Scripture that teach this doctrine.

Psalm 40:6–8. This psalm reveals a covenantal relationship of obedience and reward between the Father and the Son, especially as it is interpreted by the book of Hebrews. David begins by describing how God rescued him from a slimy pit from which he was unable to escape (40:1–2). He gives praise to God for his salvation and declares that the one who trusts in the Lord is blessed (40:3–5). Then, in verses 6–8, he makes an intriguing statement about the proper relationship between the Lord and the person who trusts in the Lord. "In sacrifice and offering you have not delighted . . . Burnt offering and sin offering you have not required. Then I said, 'Behold, I have come; in the scroll of the book it is written of me: I delight to do your will, O my God; your law is within my heart.'" It is not the sacrifices of animals in which God delights, but obedience to his commands.

Although David wrote this psalm, the writer to the Hebrews explicitly identifies the speaker in verses 6–8 as Christ. In Hebrews 10:5–10, after explaining how the sacrifices of the Mosaic covenant were inadequate to provide salvation, the writer says that Christ came into the world to do the Father's will. Psalm 40:6–8 is essentially Christ's loyal words to the Father as he submitted himself to the conditions of the covenant of redemption. The writer then makes the point that "by that will we have been sanctified through the offering of the body of Jesus Christ once for all" (10:10). Because Christ fulfilled the will of the Father through his active obedience, he has saved us and reconciled us to the Father. He satisfied the conditions of the covenant of redemption and, consequently, earned the promised reward.

Psalm 110. In this psalm, which is frequently quoted in the New Testament, the psalmist foretells of Christ's exaltation and kingship. He describes the Messiah as receiving the reward for his active obedience; he sits at the right hand of the Father (110:1) and rules in the midst of his enemies (110:2). Yet the psalmist also describes the Father's oath to the Son, "The LORD has sworn and will not change his mind, 'You are a priest forever after the order of Melchizedek'" (v. 4). As we noted in the introduction, the taking of oaths is an important aspect of covenant-making throughout Scripture. The Abrahamic and Mosaic covenants, for example, were both sealed with oaths. The same is true of the covenant of redemption between the Father and the Son. Psalm 110:4 highlights the oath-bound character of this covenant. The Father seals the covenant with his oath and designates the Son as the mediating priest for the elect.

Once more, the book of Hebrews teaches this more clearly. It explicitly interprets Psalm 110:4 in covenantal terms. In Hebrews 7, the writer compares Christ to Melchizedek in order to persuade his Hebrew-Christian audience of Christ's rightful claim to the office of high priest, even though he descended from the tribe of Judah and not from the priestly tribe of Levi. Knowing that his readers were tempted to abandon the faith and return to Judaism, he makes the argument that if perfection could come through the Levitical priesthood, there would be no reason for a greater high priest to arise after the order of Melchizedek, as foretold in Psalm 110. Applying 110:4 to Christ, he says, "For it is witnessed of him, 'You are a priest forever after the order of Melchizedek'" (7:17). He then highlights the fact that this appointment to the office of priest was with an oath: "And it was not without an oath. For those who formerly became priests were made such without an oath, but this one was made a priest with an oath by the one who said to him: 'The Lord has sworn and will not change his mind, "You are a priest forever"'" (7:20–21).

But when did this event occur? Scripture reveals no particular point in Christ's earthly ministry in which the Father made this oath to the Son. Nor is there anywhere in the Old Testament where such an oath was made. We might note that in Hebrews 7:28 the writer makes reference to the fact that Psalm 110:4 was written long after the Mosaic Law was given at Sinai, and that this "word of the oath, which came later than the law, appoints a Son who has been made perfect forever." Yet the *word* of the oath was revealed in the days of David the psalm-writer, not the oath itself. The Father made this oath to the Son when he gave him his priestly assignment in the covenant of redemption.

Isaiah 53. This well-known prophecy about the suffering Servant also teaches us about the covenant of redemption by telling us that the relationship between the Father and the Son concerning the redemption of sinners is *covenantal* in nature; it has a relationship of obedience and reward. This is revealed even in his title, "my servant" (Isa. 52:13; 53:11), which is classic covenant terminology. (For example, in Isaiah 42:1–9, the Servant is explicitly called "a covenant for the people." See also Isaiah 49:1–8.) Isaiah 53 not only foretells of the humiliation and anguish Christ experienced in his life and death but also of how his obedience to the will of the Father is the cause and basis of our redemption. After describing how Christ would be "crushed for our iniquities" (53:5) under the weight of God's wrath as our sin was imputed to him (53:6), Isaiah says in verse 10, "Yet it was the will of the LORD to crush him," and "the will of the LORD shall prosper in his hand." In other words, the suffering of Christ was according to the Father's will and, through Christ's obedience to the Father's will, his will was accomplished. This was not a haphazard or random idea; rather, this was a predetermined plan between the Father and the Son that resulted in the salvation of the elect. As Isaiah says in verse 11, it was through Christ's obedience that he made "many to be accounted righteous." His active obedience to the Father achieved the justification of his people.

The New Testament makes clear that this was a mutual agreement between the Father and the Son. Paul tells us in Philippians 2 that Christ, "though he was in the form of God, did not count equality with God a thing to be grasped, but made himself nothing, taking the form of a servant, being born in the likeness of men. And being found in human form, he humbled himself by becoming obedient to the point of death, even death on a cross" (2:6–8). The Son was not forced into this plan of redemption. He did not go unwillingly to the cross. Rather, the Father gave him work to do, and he, in turn, submitted himself to the Father's will and obeyed it perfectly.

That this was a *reward* for Christ's obedience is explicit in Isaiah 53:12: "Therefore I will divide him a portion with the many, and he shall divide the spoil with the strong." Because Christ accomplished the work the Father gave him to do, he earned the reward of a conqueror and the right to the spoils of war. The use of the word "therefore" indicates that Christ's obedience (previously described in 53:1–11) has the consequence of a reward. Paul reflects this also in Philippians 2, where he goes on to say, "Therefore God has highly exalted him and bestowed on him the name that is above every name, so that at the name of Jesus every knee should bow, in heaven and on earth and under the earth, and every tongue should confess that Jesus Christ is Lord, to the glory of God the Father" (2:9–11). Christ's reward for his obedience was the justification of his people *and* the exaltation of his name, all of which is to the glory of the Father.

Thus, Isaiah 53, in the light of the New Testament, teaches us that our redemption is the result of Christ fulfilling the conditions and receiving the reward prescribed in a pact between him and the Father.

Zechariah 6:12–13. Prophesying of the Messiah, whom he calls "the Branch," a title also used by Isaiah and Jeremiah (see Isa. 4:2; 11:1 and Jer. 23:5; 33:15), Zechariah says that "he shall build the temple of the LORD and bear royal honor, and shall sit and rule on his throne." Like Psalm 110 and Isaiah 53, this passage emphasizes the Messiah's reward for his accomplished work. It also describes the covenant that stipulated the conditions for this reward as "the counsel of peace" between Yahweh and the Branch, that is, between the Father and the Son. This phrase has covenantal connotations, for Scripture connects the making of a covenant between two or more parties to their taking counsel with one another. For example, Genesis 21:22–34 tells us of Abraham and Abimelech conversing with each other as part of their mutual covenant. Each man made stipulations of the other, and each man swore an oath to the other, promising to uphold his end of the agreement. What Scripture explicitly describes as a covenant between them (Gen. 21:27, 32) included their joint counsel. Likewise, Psalm 83:5 speaks of God's enemies as taking counsel with each other in order to make a covenant: "For they conspire with one accord; against you they make a covenant." Given the context of Zechariah's statement, "the counsel of peace" seems to be a reference to the covenant of redemption.[1]

The Gospel of John. John provides ample evidence of the covenant of redemption in his Gospel. He records Christ's many references to the work he came to accomplish, work that the Father assigned to him. For example, in chapter 4, when speaking to his disciples, he says, "My food is to do the will of him who sent me and to accomplish his work" (4:34). Then in chapter 5, when speaking to the Jewish leaders, he states,

> I can do nothing on my own. As I hear, I judge, and my judgment is just because I seek not my own will but the will of him who sent me ... For the works that the Father has given me to accomplish, the very works that I am doing, bear witness about me that the Father has sent me ... I have come in my Father's name (5:30, 36b, 43a).

Likewise, in 6:37–40, when speaking to the multitudes, he says, "All that the Father gives me will come to me, and whoever comes to me I will never cast out. For I have come down from heaven, not to do my own will but the will of him who sent me. And this is the will of him who sent me, that I should lose nothing of all that he has given me." And in 10:18, when speaking to the Pharisees, announces, "No one takes [my life] from me, but I lay it down of my own accord. I have

---

1. For more on how Zechariah 6:12–13 reveals the covenant of redemption, see Meredith Kline, *Glory in Our Midst: A Biblical-Theological Reading of Zechariah's Night Visions* (Eugene: Wipf & Stock, 2001).

authority to lay it down, and I have authority to take it up again. This charge I have received from my Father." (See also 12:49; 14:31a; and 15:10.) These comments by Jesus clearly reveal his mission on earth as *work* the Father commanded him to accomplish. In 10:18, Christ says he received a charge from the Father. The Greek word used here indicates a mandate or a command to fulfill. This mandate required him to accomplish redemption for those whom the Father gave to him by actively obeying the Father's commands, which included going to the cross to lay down his life as the propitiation for their sins.

Christ makes this most clear in his High Priestly Prayer prayed on the night before his crucifixion:

> Father, the hour has come; glorify your Son that the Son may glorify you, since you have given him authority over all flesh, to give eternal life to all whom you have given him . . . I glorified you on earth, having accomplished the work you gave me to do. And now, Father, glorify me in your own presence with the glory that I had with you before the world existed (John 17:1b-2, 4-5).

Throughout this prayer, Jesus refers to those whom the Father "gave" to him (that is, the elect in Christ) at least seven times (17:2, 6a, 6b, 9, 10, 11, 24). His mission was to save them through his obedience to the will of the Father. The next day, as he hung on the cross and suffered the wrath of God for the sins of those whom the Father gave to him, his last words were, "It is finished" (19:30). *What* was finished? The work the Father gave him to do before the foundation of the world.

Taken together, Jesus' comments in John's Gospel about the work he came to accomplish reveal a mutual, predetermined plan between the Father and the Son made in eternity past.

Ephesians 1:3-14. The opening to Paul's epistle to the Ephesians supports the notion that the Son received his charge from the Father before the foundation of the world. After his initial salutation in the first two verses, the apostle bursts forth in praise to God for his grace:

> Blessed be the God and Father of our Lord Jesus Christ, who has blessed us in Christ with every spiritual blessing in the heavenly places, even as he chose us in him before the foundation of the world, that we should be holy and blameless before him. In love

he predestined us for adoption through Jesus Christ, according to the purpose of his will, to the praise of his glorious grace, with which he has blessed us in the Beloved (1:3–6).

He makes clear that the triune God drew up the blueprint for our redemption in eternity past. He says we were chosen *in Christ* "before the foundation of the world" and predestined for adoption *through Christ*, all according to God's original plan, that is, "the purpose of his will." The Father and the Son entered into covenant with each other in order to bring sinners to glory. Out of a fallen and condemned mass of humanity, the Father chose sinners who were no more deserving or qualified to be saved than those he did not choose. He chose them in Christ *unconditionally* and according to his own purpose. As Paul says in 2 Timothy 1:9, God "saved us and called us to a holy calling, not because of our works but because of his own purpose and grace, which he gave us in Christ before the ages began." The Father gave these elect sinners to the Son, who redeemed them through his blood and provided them with complete forgiveness for all their trespasses (Eph. 1:7). The life, death, and resurrection of Christ makes known to us "the mystery of [God's] will," that is, it reveals the outworking of the covenant of redemption (1:8–10).

Yet Paul tells us that there is more to this plan. Not only did the Father elect a people in the Son but he also elected them through the Spirit. As the third person in the Godhead, the Holy Spirit has a unique role in the covenant of redemption and works to bring it to pass (1:11–12). Whereas the Son had the responsibility of *accomplishing* redemption for those whom the Father gave to him, the Spirit has the responsibility of *applying* redemption to this same people. The Spirit who prepared the way under the old covenant for the coming of Christ and supplied Christ in his incarnation with the gifts necessary to fulfill his office as Mediator, also applies to the elect the salvific benefits that Christ earned for them. He proceeds from the Father and the Son in order to unite them to Christ and seal to them all the blessings of Christ's finished work: regeneration, faith, justification, adoption, sanctification, preservation, and glorification (1:13–14; cf. John 14:26; 15:26; 16:7). He is Christ's Gift to the church, the down payment and guarantee of their promised inheritance.

Romans 5:12–19. In this passage, Paul teaches us explicit analogy between Adam and Christ, showing that both of these individuals were federal representatives of other people. Whereas Adam's *disobedience* in the covenant of works resulted in the *condemnation* of those whom he represented (that is, the whole human race), Christ's *obedience* in the covenant of redemption resulted in the *justification* of those whom he represented (that is, the elect). Again, we are confronted with scriptural teaching of the obedience-reward relationship between the Father and Son. The Son obeyed the Father so that "the many will be made righteous" (5:19; cf. 1 Cor. 15:21–22).

Other passages referring to the Father. In addition to the passages noted above, the Bible is replete with references to the Father's role in the covenant of redemption. The Father promised the Son to support him in the execution of his work (Isa. 42:1–7; 50:5–9). He promised not to abandon Christ's soul to Sheol or let his body see corruption (Ps. 16:10; 49:15; 86:13; Acts 2:31–32; Heb. 13:20). He promised the Son that, on the completion of his work, he would be exalted as King (Ps. 2:6–8; Luke 22:29; Heb. 1:1–13; 5:5–6). He promised the Son that those whom he gave to him would serve him, proclaim his righteousness, and tell future generations of his accomplished work (Ps. 22:30–31).

Other passages referring to the Son. Scripture teaches us that the Son is the covenant Mediator who is also one with Father (Gal. 3:15–22). He was sent by the Father on a specific mission (Matt. 10:40; 15:24; 21:37; Luke 4:18, 43; 10:16). He submitted himself to the Father's will and did not turn back (Isa. 50:5–9). He learned obedience through what he suffered (Heb. 5:8). He endured the cross to which he was appointed, even though he despised the shame associated with it (Heb. 12:2). He made known the mystery of God's will which was kept hidden from eternity past (Eph. 3:8–12).

Other passages referring to the Holy Spirit. As a member of the triune Godhead, the Holy Spirit always acts in concert with the Father and the Son, and the Father and Son never act apart from the Spirit. Passages that refer to his acting in the incarnation and resurrection of Christ, as well as his work of uniting the elect with Christ, are not incidental to Christ's work. Rather, they should be understood as the fulfillment of the Spirit's role in the covenant of redemption. The Scriptures clearly reveal that the Spirit caused the Son to assume a real human nature by the Virgin Mary (Matt. 1:18; Luke 1:35, 80). It was through the Spirit that Christ offered himself to the Father (Heb. 9:14). And it was the Spirit who caused Christ to be raised from the dead (Rom. 8:11). Without the Spirit fulfilling these critical tasks, the covenant of redemption would never have been accomplished.

All the evidence above leads us to conclude with Owen, Witsius, and the Reformed tradition that Scripture teaches a pretemporal, intratrinitarian covenant between the divine persons for the redemption of the elect. The relationship between the Father and the Son is characterized by the obedience-reward pattern. As we noted in the introduction, there is always a legal aspect to covenantal relations. They are simultaneously *personal* and *legal*. This is true not only in covenants common to us today, such as the covenant of marriage between one man and one woman, but also in biblical covenants, whether entered jointly (as in the case of Abraham's covenant with Abimelech in Gen. 21:22–34) or unilaterally imposed (as in the case of the covenant of works with Adam in Gen. 2:8–16). The obedience-reward pattern of the Father and Son involves the legal nature the covenant of redemption. Christ's reward of a kingdom and redeemed people was conditioned on his obedience.

What Does Reformed Theology Teach?

The Westminster Confession of Faith (1647) alludes to the covenant of redemption when it says, "It pleased God, in His eternal purpose, to choose and ordain the Lord Jesus, His only begotten Son, to be Mediator between God and man" (8.1). The Savoy Declaration of Faith (1658), which was a modification of the Westminster Confession by English Independents, made this even more explicit: "It pleased God, in his eternal purpose, to choose and ordain the Lord Jesus, His only begotten Son, *according to a Covenant made between them both*, to be the Mediator between God and Man" (8.1, emphasis added). Historically, Reformed theology has taught that the mediation of Christ was the outworking of the covenant of redemption.

What exactly was included in this covenant? John Owen (1616–83), one of the chief architects of the Savoy Declaration and often called the "Prince of the Puritans," described the covenant of redemption as having five major elements:

1. The Father as "promiser" and the Son as "undertaker" voluntarily agreed together in counsel to achieve a common purpose, namely, "the glory of God and the salvation of the elect."[2]

2. The Father prescribed conditions for this covenant, which consisted of the Son assuming human nature, fulfilling the demands of the law through his obedience, and suffering the just judgment of God for the elect in order to satisfy God's justice on their behalf.[3]

3. The Father promised the Son that he would support him, and that if the Son accomplished the work given to him, he would achieve salvation and glorification for the elect. The Father confirmed these promises with an oath.[4]

4. The Son voluntarily accepted the conditions, and assumed the work as surety of the covenant.[5]

5. The Father approved and accepted the performance of the Son, who likewise laid claim to the promises made in the covenant.[6]

This summary is typical among Reformed theologians of the seventeenth century. They understood Scripture to teach the covenant of redemption as one of obedience and obligation *for Christ*. Forgiveness of sins and eternal life for the elect was possible only by Christ fulfilling the demands of God's justice through his life of obedience and death of atonement. Thus, Christ became the covenant-keeper in whom we place our trust for salvation.

---

2. *Vindiciae Evangelicae; or, The Mystery of the Gospel Vindicated and Socinianism Examined* (1655), in *Works*, vol. 12 (Edinburgh: Banner of Truth, repr.1998), 498–500. Owen cited Prov. 8:22–31; Ps. 60:14; Isaiah 9:6; Zech. 4:12–13; 13:7; Heb. 2:9–10; 12:2.

3. *Works*, 12:499, 501–2. Owen cited Job 33:23, 24; Isa. 42:1; 49:5; 53:10; John 14:28; Rom. 8:3; Gal. 4:4; Phil. 2:6–7; Heb. 10:5–9. See also *Works*, 10:168–174; 22:446–481.

4. *Works*, 12:499, 503–5. Owen cited Ps 16:10–11; 22:30–31; 89:27–28; Isa. 42:4, 6; 50:5–9; 52.1–4; 53:10,11; Heb. 5:7; 7:21, 28; 12:2.

5. *Works*, 12:499, 505. Owen cited Ps. 16.2; 40.7–8; Isa. 50:5; Phil. 2:6–8.

6. *Works*, 12:499, 505–507. Owen cited Job 33:24; Ps. 2:7–8; Isa. 49:5–9; Dan. 9:24; Acts 13:33; Rom. 1:4; Jn. 17; Heb. 7:25, 9:24.

Owen also pointed out that the Holy Spirit has an essential role in the covenant of redemption. It was through the Holy Spirit that the Virgin Mary conceived the incarnate Christ, Christ offered himself to the Father, and he was raised from the dead.[7] Moreover, the Holy Spirit is also responsible for bringing the elect into union with Christ and keeping them secure.[8] Our salvation is Trinitarian from beginning to end.

British theologians, however, were not the only ones to explain the covenant of redemption in this way. Most European Reformed theologians held to the same teaching. The Dutch Reformed theologian Herman Witsius (1636-1708) described it as

> the will of the Father, giving the Son to be the Head and Redeemer of the elect; and the will of the Son, presenting himself as a Sponsor or Surety for them; in all which the nature of a compact and agreement consists. The scriptures represent the Father, in the economy of our salvation, as demanding the obedience of the Son even unto death; and upon condition of that obedience, promising him in his turn that name which is above every name, even that he should be the head of the elect in glory; but the Son, as presenting himself to do the will of the Father, acquiescing in that promise, and . . . requiring, by virtue of the compact, the kingdom and glory promised to him. When we have clearly demonstrated all these particulars from scripture, it cannot, on any pretence be denied, that there is a compact between the Father and the Son which is the foundation of our salvation.[9]

Like Owen, Witsius explained this covenant as having prescribed conditions, which the Son voluntarily agreed to fulfill. To save sinners and yet at the same time have his justice satisfied against sin, the Father required the Son to take the place of the elect by becoming the second Adam and fulfilling all righteousness through his obedience. The Son agreed, fulfilled the conditions, and received his reward of a kingdom and glory with his redeemed people.

---

7. 10:163-78. Owen referred to Mt. 1:18; Lk. 1:35, 80; Rom. 1:4; 8:11; Heb. 9:14; and 1 Pet. 3:18.

8. 11:336ff.

9. Herman Witsius, *The Economy of the Covenants between God & Man*, 2 vols., (1693, trans. William Crookshank, 1822; repr. Escondido: The den Dulk Foundation, 1990), 1:166.

Reformed theology has typically described Christ's role in the covenant of redemption with terms such as *federal head, mediator* (for example, Heb. 8:6; 9:15; 12:24) and *surety* (for example, Heb. 7:22). These titles generally refer to the same concept, namely, Christ as the representative of his people, yet each emphasizes different aspects of this role. The expression *federal head* highlights the fact that Christ is a public person who acts on behalf of those whom he represents. To borrow an example used by S. M. Baugh, "when the President of the United States signs a treaty, it binds all the citizens he represents to uphold that treaty. Should the President break the treaty through his official actions, the whole country may be accountable."[10] In like manner, Christ's actions have consequences for the elect, for he is their federal head. The word *mediator,* on the other hand, draws attention to Christ representing us before the Father in his threefold office of Prophet, Priest, and King. Additionally, the title *surety* stresses Christ as the guarantee of our salvation, who fulfilled the conditions of his covenant with the Father.

Why Is This Doctrine Important for the Christian Life?

Why should the Christian care that there was a covenant of redemption between the Father, Son, and Holy Spirit before time? At first glance, we might be tempted to think of this doctrine as rather abstract and impractical, as if it only has value in the seminary classroom or the speculative conversations of professional theologians. Nothing, however, could be further from the truth. The doctrine of the covenant of redemption is indeed *very* practical for the Christian life, for it teaches us about the love of God, provides us with comfort and assurance, and guards us against speculation.

It teaches us about the love of God. The doctrine of the covenant of redemption reveals to us that there exists between the Father, Son, and Holy Spirit perfect love and harmony. Their promises and commitments *to* each other demonstrate their love *for* each other. The Father's love for the Son is expressed in his reward of a people whom the Son will rule as King. The Son's love for the Father is

---

10. S.M. Baugh, "Covenant Theology Illustrated: Romans 5 on the Federal Headship of Adam and Christ," *Modern Reformation*, v01.9, n0.4, July/August 2000.

expressed in his submission to the Father's will, even at the highest personal cost. The Spirit's love for the Father and the Son is expressed in his work to bring this plan to completion. And the Father and Son's love for the Spirit is expressed in pouring him out on the church as their special gift from heaven. No member of the Trinity acts apart from the other two members.

Yet the doctrine of the covenant of redemption also teaches us that God is eternally moved to communicate to others this love that he experiences within himself. As the Old Princeton theologian Geerhardus Vos (1862-1949) put it, "Just as the blessedness of God exists in the free relationship of the three persons of the adorable Being, so man shall also find his blessedness in the covenantal relationship with his God."[11] God has decided to share his love with his elect. In his sovereign will, he chose to make us the objects of the eternal, mutual love between the Father, Son, and Holy Spirit. We did nothing to move him to this love, for he loved us while we were still sinners and his enemies (Rom. 5:8-10). Rather, he acted first by setting his love on us before the foundation of the world in this great covenant involving each person of the Godhead. In the covenant of redemption, we see that our salvation is Trinitarian from beginning to end, carefully planned in eternity past and executed in human history. What amazing love is demonstrated by the fact that Christ came on a specific mission to fulfill his covenant obligations and obtain redemption for us!

It provides us with comfort and assurance. Knowing that our salvation was planned out by the triune God before the foundation of the world gives us unspeakable comfort. If you are a Christian, it is because the Father, Son, and Holy Spirit covenanted together in eternity to save you. You are not a Christian because you are better, smarter, or possess a softer heart than other people. You are a Christian because the Father chose you in the Son, the Son fulfilled the conditions for your salvation, and the Spirit applied to you the redemptive benefits of the Son's work. When you are tempted to doubt your salvation, remember that Christ said, "It

---

11. Geerhardus Vos, *Redemptive History and Biblical Interpretation: The Shorter Writings of Geerhardus Vos* (Phillipsburg: P & R, 1980), 245.

is finished," and that the Father is satisfied with the work of his Son. Your salvation remains secure, not because of anything *you* do, but because Christ finished the work the Father gave him to accomplish and satisfied God's justice. Consequently, the Father has highly exalted him. <u>The obedience-reward pattern in the covenant of redemption causes us to look to Christ rather than ourselves for assurance of our salvation.</u>

Here's how Louis Berkhof explains it:

> Though the covenant of redemption is the eternal basis of the covenant of grace, and as far as sinners are concerned, also its eternal prototype, <u>it was for Christ a covenant of works rather than a covenant of grace. For him the law of the original covenant applied, namely, that eternal life could only be obtained by meeting the demands of the law.</u> As the last Adam, Christ obtains eternal life for sinners in reward for faithful obedience, and not at all as an unmerited gift of grace. And what he has done as the Representative and Surety of all his people, they are no more in duty bound to do. The work has been done, the reward is merited, and believers are made partakers of the fruits of Christ's accomplished work through grace.[12]

<u>That Christ earned our redemption as the reward for his faithful work comforts us, for it assures us that we are saved by *his* merit and not our own.</u> We are acceptable to the Father not because of *our* obedience, but because of *his* obedience. As Heidelberg Catechism Question 60 puts it,

> Although my conscience accuses me, that I have grievously sinned against all the commandments of God, and have never kept any of them, and am still prone always to all evil; yet God, without any merit of mine, of mere grace, grants and imputes to me the perfect satisfaction, righteousness, and holiness of Christ, as if I had never committed nor had any sins, and had myself accomplished all the obedience which Christ has fulfilled for me; if only I accept such benefit with a believing heart.

The doctrine of the covenant of redemption highlights the obedience of Christ as our legal representative and the merit he

---

12. Louis Berkhof, *Systematic Theology* (Grand Rapids: Eerdmans, 1996), 268.

earned for us in our place. What comfort this brings us as those who are often find ourselves troubled in conscience by the weakness of our faith and our failures in the Christian life!

It guards us against speculation. Although some might be concerned that the doctrine of the covenant of redemption is speculative in nature, it actually guards us against speculation. Not only is it founded on strong biblical evidence but it also sets forth Christ in his person and work as the object of our faith. Rather than leading us to speculate about the hidden decrees of God (which we are prone to do by our sinful nature), this doctrine leads us to look no further than our Mediator, who came in human flesh to live, die, and be raised again from the dead. As Michael Horton says, "God's predestination is hidden to us, but Christ is not. The unveiling of the mystery hidden in past ages, the person and work of Christ, becomes the only reliable testimony to our election. Those who trust in Christ belong to Christ, are elect in Christ."[13] The doctrine of the covenant of redemption safeguards this revelation. It tells us to look to the One who is our covenant Surety and Mediator, who has secured for us the blessings of redemption, faith, justification, adoption, sanctification, preservation, and glorification. It tells us, as pilgrims traveling in this present evil age, to keep our eyes fixed on the Author and Finisher of our faith, the One who obeyed the Father in all things. It tells us that, though life is messy, unpredictable, and filled with suffering, we have a salvation that will not change or fade away, for it was earned for us by the Lord of glory himself.

Questions for Further Reflection

1. What is unique about the covenant of redemption? How is it different from other biblical covenants?
2. What was the role of the Father in the covenant of redemption?
3. What was the role of the Son in the covenant of redemption?
4. What is the role of the Spirit in the covenant of redemption?
5. How does the doctrine of the covenant of redemption comfort you?

---

13. Michael Horton, *God of Promise* (Grand Rapids: Baker, 2002), 79.

Failure in Paradise:
THE COVENANT OF WORKS

"For God so loved the world, that he gave his only Son, that whoever believes in him should not perish but have eternal life" (John 3:16). "Repent and be baptized every one of you in the name of Jesus Christ for the forgiveness of your sins" (Acts 2:38). These are classic verses that summarize the gospel. They proclaim the good news to us about how we can be saved from our sin.

These verses, and others like them, hold a dear place in our hearts. The gospel comforts us in times of doubt, and it encourages us when we are weary. We sometimes cross-stitch these verses to hang on our wall, make them the background on our computer, and tape them up in our workplace. They are comforting reminders of the great salvation that we have in Christ. And yet these verses raise the question: How this can be? How is it possible for depraved sinners to be saved merely through faith? Why did Christ have to die on the cross? What did Christ do so that we could have eternal life by believing in him? What is necessary for sinful man to be redeemed?

In answer to these questions, we may first go to one of Paul's epistles or to a passage in the gospels; we could certainly find the answer there. There is another place, however, to which one can turn to find answers to these very questions, namely, the opening chapters of Genesis. This may come as a surprise to some of us. We understand how important the first few chapters of Genesis are with respect to creation. But how do they preach the gospel?

The apostolic preaching of the gospel is the bridge that brings us to God as Savior; it is paved and clearly marked. But the pillars on this bridge, which are rooted deep into the riverbed below, belong to Genesis 1–3. The streaming water may hide the pillars from our eyes at times; yet, without the Genesis pillars, the gospel viaduct would begin crumbling beneath our feet, hurling us headfirst into the water.

Genesis 1–3 forms the essential foundation for the gospel, especially because it reveals the covenant of works. The doctrine of the covenant of works teaches us more about the perfect work of Christ and, in so doing, bolsters up our assurance of salvation.

What Is the Covenant of Works?

The doctrine of the covenant of works has a distinguished pedigree. While the concept of a covenant of works is found in writings as early as Augustine (354–430), robust formulations of the doctrine were taught in the time of the Reformation by theologians such as Zacharias Ursinus (1534–83) and Caspar Olevianus (1536–87), authors of the Heidelberg Catechism (1563). In his Larger Catechism (1562), Ursinus explicitly equated the covenant of works to the law, which "requires our perfect obedience to God" and "promises eternal life to those who keep it," and equated the covenant of grace to the gospel, which "shows us the fulfillment in Christ of the righteousness that the law requires" and "promises eternal life freely because of Christ to those who believe in him."[1] Olevianus taught the same doctrine in his 1567 *Vester Grund*. He spoke of a legal covenant of works with Adam as the federal head of humanity, in whom the law was "implanted" as a matter of "human nature."[2] This covenant of works stands in contrast to the covenant of grace, which declares the "Surety who completely satisfies the just judgment of God for us."[3]

---

1. Zacharias Ursinus, *Larger Catechism*, Q.36, as found in Lyle Bierma et al., *An Introduction to the Heidelberg Catechism: Sources, History, and Theology*, Texts and Studies in Reformation and Post-Reformation Thought (Grand Rapids: Baker, 2005), 168–69.

2. Caspar Olevianus, *A Firm Foundation. An Aid to Interpreting the Heidelberg Catechism*, trans. Lyle D. Bierma, Texts and Studies in Reformation and Post-Reformation Thought (Grand Rapids: Baker Books, 1995), 3–5.

3. Olevianus, *Firm Foundation*, 3.

By the 1640s, the doctrine of the covenant of works was officially recognized and codified in the confessional standards produced by the Westminster Assembly. The Westminster Shorter Catechism (WSC), for example, defines this covenant as follows: "When God had created man, he entered into a covenant of life with him, upon condition of perfect obedience; forbidding him to eat of the tree of the knowledge of good and evil, upon pain of death" (Q&A 12). Likewise the Westminster Confession of Faith (WCF) asserts, "The first covenant made with man was a covenant of works, wherein life was promised to Adam; and in him to his posterity, upon condition of perfect and personal obedience" (7.2). Consistent with these statements, Louis Berkhof says that the covenant of works is God's commitment to Adam, as Federal Head, wherein life is conditioned on perfect obedience, and [eternal] death is threatened upon the disobedience of eating the forbidden fruit.[4]

There are four aspects of this definition that are helpful for us to flesh out a bit. *First, God is the one who made the covenant, and he did so at creation.* For Adam and Eve to be made in the image of God is for them to be in covenant with God. At creation, God commits himself to his creation to sustain them and be God to them. So also, being created in the image of God by necessity obligates Adam to God. In Genesis 1:26, God fashions male and female in his image so that they may have dominion, which is an obligation. God's act of creation generates a relationship with implicit obligations, namely, to imitate God. God's covenantal commitment to his human creations, then, is evident in Genesis 1, even before the narrower command not to eat of the Tree of Knowledge of Good and Evil. This prohibition focuses the covenant relationship on a specific test, but the covenant is bigger than this one command.

Second, the promise of life everlasting is based on Adam's obedience. His works were the means of obtaining the promise. Adam's righteous deeds would have earned him the reward, and his obedience had to be perfect and perpetual. Adam could have sinned in other ways than eating from the forbidden tree. To image God is to be perfectly righteous continually.

---

4. *Systematic Theology*, (Grand Rapids: Eerdmans, 1996), 215–17.

A common objection to this idea is the question of how Adam's work could merit anything from God. Surely, a human being could never earn something from God so that God owed it to him? But this objection misses the fact that God is sovereign to set the terms. He created and called it good. So also, he is free to assign the value of goods. The exchange rate is in his hands. Man will earn from God what God says he will earn. This is not because there is anything intrinsically meritorious in humanity, but because of God's word. Therefore, the Lord is sovereign to declare the value of eternal life, and he valued it at the price of perfect obedience. It was a covenantally determined merit. The Lord determined the terms of the covenant, and his justice will make sure that it is upheld.

Furthermore, God created man with the ability to succeed. God fashioned Adam and Eve in true righteousness and holiness (Eph. 4:24). Sin was not yet in the picture. The Lord made Adam righteous, so that he was naturally inclined to obedience. It was his delight, his first inclination, his natural demeanor. So the Belgic Confession says that Adam was "capable in all things to will agreeably to the will of God" (Art. 14); and the Heidelberg Catechism, "God so made man that he could perform [His law]" (Q&A 9). Adam was able perfectly and perpetually to obey God for the reward of life everlasting.

Third, the blessing/reward and the curse/punishment of the covenant were ultimately eternal and spiritual in nature. The life promised was eternal life. The Tree of Life was a sign and guarantee to Adam that if he obeyed he would live forever. Hence, God bars Adam and Eve from the Tree of Life, lest they eat and live forever (Gen. 3:22). John Calvin (1509–64) states this clearly in his discussion of the sacramental character of the Tree of Life, "[God] gave Adam and Eve the tree of life as a guarantee of immortality."[5] The tree of life in the center of Eden symbolized the everlasting beatitude Adam's obedience was to earn (Rev. 22:2).

Eternal life was merited by Adam's obedience, and so eternal death was earned by his disobedience. The reward is matched by the punishment. God assigned the penalty for disobedience as death:

---

5. John Calvin, *Institutes of the Christian Religion* (1559), ed. J. T. McNeill, trans. F. L. Battles (Philadelphia: Westminster Press, repr. 1975), 4.14.18.

"In the day you eat of it, you shall surely die" (Gen. 2:17). Death here is used inclusively of physical, spiritual, and eternal death. <u>Biblically, death is not merely the end of physical existence, but it is characterized more so by separation from God and all his goodness.</u> At their fall, Adam and Eve did not physically die, but they did immediately realize their spiritual shame by becoming aware of their nakedness (Gen. 3:7). So WSC 19 states, "All mankind by their fall lost communion with God, are under his wrath and curse, and so made liable to all the miseries of this life, to death itself, and to the pains of hell forever."

Fourth, God made the covenant with Adam and all his posterity. 4. Every son of Adam and daughter of Eve is in this covenant. Adam represented and acted on behalf of them all. God appointed Adam as our federal head and legal representative.

Quite simply, this means the consequences of Adam's actions were imputed and passed on to his children. If he earned life, he earned it for himself and all his descendants, and so also with death. This aspect of the covenant is obvious from human history. Once Adam fell, death came to Eve, Cain, and Abel, even to all mankind (Rom. 5:12). Cain and Abel were not put back in the place of Adam; rather, they were exiled east of Eden. The guilt of sin was theirs, and they inherited their father's corrupt nature. And this is how it has been ever since. <u>God does not place us back to the starting line where Adam began. Instead, we are born being dead in sin</u> (Eph. 2:1–3). All of humanity, then, is in this covenant in Adam. This covenant shapes all of history; our destiny and life was determined by this covenant. We all fell in Adam and are therefore imprisoned in sin and its curse of death.

In light of these characteristics, we can define the covenant of works as *God's commitment to give Adam, and his posterity in him, eternal life for obedience or eternal death for disobedience.* It is the original state into which Adam and Eve were created. <u>Being in the image of God,</u> Adam had a righteous and holy nature, <u>wherein he was able to earn the reward by his works.</u>

Theologians have called this covenant by different names over time, but they have agreed consistently as to its character. Some called it the covenant of life, with respect to the goal of the covenant (WSC Q&A 12). Had Adam obeyed, he would have earned eternal life. Others labeled it the covenant of creation, because it was made at creation. The name covenant of works, however, highlights the means whereby Adam was going to earn eternal life; it was by his works that eternal life was to be achieved. The varying names reflect different aspects of the same covenant.

Yet the name covenant of works has come to predominate Reformed theology because this name particularly contrasts it with the covenant of grace. The covenant of grace has in common with the covenant of works that it is a covenant unto life, but how this life is attained is the key difference. In the covenant of grace, God's people receive life as a gift through faith in the perfect work of Christ our Mediator. But in the covenant of works, Adam would merit life by his obedience to the terms of the covenant. It is for this reason that covenant of works is an apt and helpful name for this covenant.

What Does the Bible Teach?

Reformed confessions and theology seek to summarize and teach what the Bible teaches. God's inspired Word is the only infallible rule for faith and life. <u>Reformed theology is covenant theology because it is exegetical theology, that is to say, it is based on and rooted in the exegesis of Scripture.</u> <u>Reformed theology teaches the covenant of works because it is found in God's Word</u>. Even though the covenant of works has been codified in the Reformed tradition, still many in other traditions do not teach the covenant of works, and a few within the Reformed tradition have taken issue with this doctrine. It is hence necessary and proper to explore those passages of Holy Scripture that teach and shed light on the covenant of works.

Genesis 2–3. The first passage should naturally be the actual account of Adam and Eve's fall. In fact, one of the more common arguments against the covenant of works is that the Scriptures do not use the term *covenant* to describe what is going on in the pre-fall state. The Genesis 2–3 narrative is void of the term *covenant*. This, of course, is true. The word *covenant* is not in Genesis 2–3. This should not, however, be a stumbling block for us.[6] In our

---

6. This also happens in 2 Samuel 7, where God does not use the term covenant in talking to David, although it is clearly a covenant.

everyday lives and throughout Scripture, we can talk about objects, topics, or things without using the explicit term or name; we can use symbols or synonyms, or the matter can merely be clear from the context. If all the stuff of a covenant is present in Genesis 2–3, the term is not needed.

Context is particularly important with common relationships. A story or movie can reveal that a man and a woman are married in all sorts of ways without using the actual terms of husband/wife or married. Synonymous terms like *hitched* or *better-half* could be used, or the marriage relationship could be shown by the way the man and woman converse. The simple picture of an older couple walking and holding hands can demonstrate marriage. Likewise, the covenantal character of Genesis 2–3 is equally clear from the narrative context.

However, every context has a learning curve. If you are visiting at a friend's house, you may have had no exposure to the sayings or phrases his family uses for certain things. In my house, we call radishes *dirt* because when I was a kid my dad said radishes tasted like dirt. Thus, if you were not familiar with this, the dinner table request of "please pass the dirt" would be confusing. If this is the case from one family to another or one culture to another where things can be lost in translation, how much more for a culture that is roughly three thousand years old? Symbols, images, and idioms vary, and so we need to learn them. What was second nature to an ancient Hebrew has a high probability of being misunderstood by us without study.

We must keep in mind that the context for the opening chapters of Genesis is Israel coming out of Egypt after God made a covenant with them at Sinai. Israel's new life after slavery in Egypt was monopolized by the covenant. <u>Moses authored these chapters, as he was carried along by the Spirit, particularly with the people of Israel in mind.</u> Thus, the terms and imagery of Genesis 2–3 should be understood in part in light of their uses elsewhere. Israel did not just receive Genesis 2–3 with nothing else; rather, these opening chapters came as part of the whole, along with the rest of the books of Genesis and Exodus through Deuteronomy.

A good example of this is the name used for God in Genesis 2–3. In these two chapters, the Lord is referred to almost exclusively as the "LORD God" (twenty times). The only exception is in chapter three, from the lips of the woman and the serpent, just "God" (four times). These variations have narrative purpose deliberately creating distance between God and the woman and the serpent. Nevertheless, "LORD God" is the covenantal name for God. It has the connotation of God being a covenantal God, one who is in a solemn relationship with his people. This designation is found in Exodus 3:14–18, when God calls Moses to deliver Israel from Egypt. In Exodus 20:2, it is used in the covenantal prologue to the Ten Commandments, and it is pervasive in Deuteronomy. The Israelites would have naturally heard covenantal overtones and obligations in this very designation the "LORD God," and so should we.

In addition to this, it must be acknowledged that the whole of Genesis 2–3 is a narrative with characters, a plot, and theme. And good narrative, especially in the Old Testament, communicates its meaning primarily through the story and not with bald side comments ("this means . . ."). The setting and development of the plot and characters are enough for the reader to make judgments. Consider what Barry Webb states about how Hebrew narrative communicates meaning, "The significance which the events had for the writer . . . is expressed by the manner in which the story is told and is never stated directly."[7] To demand an explicit "this is a covenant" line in Genesis 2–3 is to force shoddy writing on the text. With such impositions, the reader comes to the text as lord, rather than in submission to the text.

By listening to and re-reading the Genesis 2–3 narrative, it becomes evident that it is covenantal through and through, even though the term is not used. By analogy, the observation of one scholar about Genesis 2–3 would apply to the idea of covenant, "Though none of the Hebrew words for 'sin' appears in the text, the notion is very much present."[8] The idea of covenant pervades the narrative, for its theme and the story line focus us on the covenantal obligation for Adam and Eve not to eat of the Tree of Knowledge of Good and Evil. Any casual reader would pick this up. This obligation or test lies at the core of the story. And as we mentioned above in the introduction, one of the synonyms of covenant is the obligations.

---

7. Barry Webb, "*The Theme of the Jephthah Story (Judges 10:6–12:7)*" RTR 45. 2 My–Ag (1986): 34–43.

8. Tryggve N.D. Mettinger, *The Eden Narrative*, (Winona Lake: Eisenbrauns, 2007), 25.

Therefore, immediately in these opening chapters, Adam and the Tree of Knowledge are front and center in the narrative. In 2:8, God plants Eden and places the man in it; then in verse 9, God causes the good and pleasant trees to grow along with the Tree of Knowledge and the Tree of Life. These two trees are listed as being in the midst of the garden right at the beginning of the description of Eden. The whole garden looks into and flows out from these two trees. Their prominence in the Edenic geography foreshadows narrative significance. Place connotes worth.

In 2:15, the narrative recalls verse 8, where God places Adam in Eden, and along with such placement comes duty. Adam's privileged post in paradise brings the responsibility to serve and guard the garden. Next, in the first direct speech of the story, the Lord issues the command for Adam not to eat of the Tree of Knowledge. As we might expect, those trees rooted in Eden's nucleus are back on stage, the Tree of Knowledge being in the forefront. In fact, the Hebrew word for *knowledge* can also mean "choosing," the act of knowledge instead of the state of knowledge. This tree may be better named the "Tree of Choosing Good and Evil."[9] This prohibition colors the Tree of Knowledge as a test. The specific prohibition, with its somewhat arbitrary character, combined with the name of the tree raises the question in the reader: Will Adam choose good or evil by obeying God's word?

The prominence and significance of the Tree of Knowledge also by default sheds light on the Tree of Life. If the Tree of Knowledge is one of testing, with the penalty of death, then with a name like "Tree of Life," the other tree symbolizes the reward. One tree leads to death and the other to life. And this value of the Tree of Life is borne out at the end of the Eden narrative. Adam and Eve's rebellion results in God barring them from it with flaming swords.

Once the woman is created, the conflict in the story arises in chapter 3. The serpent is introduced, and his temptation is set forth explicitly in terms that we expect: concerning the Tree of Knowledge and God's prohibition. The Tree of Knowledge is evidently a testing tree, a tree of probation. Will Adam and Eve show allegiance and

---

9. See Geerhardus Vos's discussion of this in his *Biblical Theology* (Carlisle, PA: Banner of Truth Trust, 1996), 30–32.

submission to God above all else? Will they trust their own eyes or God's word? It appeared to them that the tree was good for food, but God assigned to it by his word the value of death. To eat was not to be fed but to be deserving of death.

The narrative test is balanced with blessing and curse, life and death. With God's voice from Sinai still ringing in Israel's ears, the command not to eat, with sanctions, is covenantal. Adam was in a covenant with God in which obedience leads to life and disobedience to death. Even though the word for covenant is not used, a complete DNA match is found. God is the one who makes the covenant as Creator, Law-maker, and Judge. The Lord God sets the terms with sanctions, the blessing of life everlasting for obedience, and the curse of eternal death for disobedience. God gives Adam a sign or sacrament of the covenant reward in the Tree of Life, and the test is focused on a juxtaposing sign in the Tree of Knowledge of Good and Evil. So Bruce Waltke concludes, "Since Adam was the only human being who could have resisted temptation, his failure implies that humanity cannot keep covenant with God. If Adam before the Fall proved unfaithful in Paradise, how much more will Israel fail in the land when surrounded by the depraved Canaanites."[10] The Eden narrative taught Israel about the historical beginnings of the world, as it does us, but it also spiritually impressed on them their inability to keep God's law, thus casting them on God's grace and mercy. Likewise Adam's covenantal rebellion helps us cling ever closer to the grace of God in Jesus Christ, the last Adam.

There are many more details that could be mentioned that further highlight the covenant relationship between God and Adam in Genesis 2–3 (see Appendix 1 for suggested reading). Yet, two more will suffice for our present purpose in order to demonstrate how Genesis 2–3 clearly teaches the covenant of works. The first has to do with the eternal character of the promise. It is not uncommon for some to doubt that Adam's obedience would have earned life eternal, because this is not explicitly stated in 2:17 to match the prohibition. But this is again a case where the narrative makes this clear without overtly stating it. To begin with, Adam's law-breaking earned the

---

10. Bruce K. Waltke, *Genesis* (Grand Rapids: Zondervan, 2001), 101.

penalty of death, so it is only natural to suppose the opposite, namely, that obedience merits life.

Furthermore, in God's statement in 3:22 ("lest he reach out his hand and take *also* of the Tree of Life and eat, and live forever"), the "also" points in the direction that Adam had not yet eaten of the Tree of Life. Without righteousness exercised by passing the test, he had no right to the tree, and his disobedience disqualified him from the prize. Additionally, the symbolic value of the Tree of Life points to a life greater than what Adam presently possessed. Adam was alive and well in paradise with his wife; hence, the reward for obedience had to offer him something more. It offered a confirmation of righteousness and life in which death was no longer a possibility. As long as the test remained unpassed, the possibility of failure and death hung over Adam's head. Such inviolable peace is a reward, something to be earned.

The second point is the overall setting of Genesis 2–3 in a paradise garden. As we instinctively know, the location where an action takes place has a huge effect on it. If a child throws a ball, it makes all the difference if this is in a ball field, in church, or in a glass shop. The same throwing action that is applauded on the ball field is deserving of discipline in a church, and the police could even get involved if it was in a glass shop. Likewise, the fact that Eden is a place where God dwells cannot be overlooked. By definition in the ancient Near East, temples were houses of gods, dwellings of the gods. To go to the temple was to draw near the presence of the gods. So also, the tabernacle and temple of the Old Testament was the place of God's name, upon which God's presence descended in the Glory-cloud (see Ex. 40:34–35 and 1 Kings 8:10–11). God dwelling in a paradise garden means that it is a holy place, a sanctuary. Holy places in the ancient world were either temples or had the attributes of a temple.

This holy temple setting, then, means that Adam was a priest. Only priests, along with their guilds of servants, lived and worked in temple precincts in the ancient world. One had to be consecrated as holy to live in a holy place. Only the priests had the security clearance to enter the temple. Adam then was a priest. In fact, the tasks of serving and guarding given to Adam in 2:15 are the most common

Hebrew verbs used for what the Aaronic priests and the Levites did in tabernacle and temple (Num. 1:53, 3:7–10).

Adam's priestly identity further reveals how he is in covenant with God. By analogy, God's promise to Aaron that the priesthood would remain always in his lineage is called a covenant (Num. 25:12–13). Moreover, the righteous purity required of priests fits that which is required of Adam to remain in God's presence forever. Positive righteousness is demanded of Adam to remain a priest of the paradise-sanctuary of God's presence.

"a covenant of peace," "of perpetual priesthood"

Ezekiel makes this garden-temple imagery and the required righteousness quite explicit in Ezekiel 28:11–19 in his lamentation for Tyre. Here, the prophet compares the king of Tyre to Adam in Eden in order to contrast Tyre's beauty with its wickedness. Ezekiel calls Tyre Eden and the garden of God (28:13); God installed the king of Tyre on the holy mountain of God (v. 14) and he created him blameless (v. 15). The jewels listed in verse 13 largely match the jewels of the high priest's breastpiece of judgment (see Ex. 28:17–20),[11] which symbolize righteousness.[12] This is an accurate comparison to Adam, a righteous priest installed in the temple garden of God. However, then unrighteousness was found in Tyre (vv. 15–16), which brought punishment. As God says, "I cast you as a profane thing from the mountain of God" (v. 16). Being in the holy garden-mountain of God carried with it the unspoken covenant obligation of righteousness and holiness. Therefore, when Tyre broke this obligation, it became unholy and had to be cast out—no longer having access to the paradise of God. Ezekiel can describe the king of Tyre in such terms because these terms were true for Adam. Eden is the original holy garden of God, which is used as metaphor to describe Tyre. Adam was the original righteous priest to whom the king of Tyre is compared. In fact, Ezekiel even matches the sin. In Ezekiel 28:2, the king of Tyre is condemned for the hubris of

The priestly connection

---

11. In the MT, nine jewels are listed in Ezekiel 28:13 all of which are found in Exodus 28:17–20; the LXX of Ezekiel 28:13 has all twelve of the same jewels found in the LXX of Exodus 28:17–20 and in the same order. So the LXX makes the priestly connection even more explicit.

12. See G.K. Beale's discussion in *The Book of Revelation* (Grand Rapids: Eerdmans, 1999), 1080–1088.

claiming, "I am a god." How well this fits Adam's arrogant rebellion where he ate to be like God (Gen. 3:5).

Ezekiel's use of Genesis 2–3 in his oracle of judgment and lamentation against the king of Tyre reveals the prophet's own exegesis of Genesis. According to Ezekiel, Eden is the holy temple-garden of God, and Adam was the beautifully righteous priest, created and installed by God in Eden. The covenantal overtones of the relationship and requirements pervade the prophet's exegesis of Genesis. Moreover, Ezekiel's comparison between Adam and the king of Tyre is fitting, for Tyre's monarch is not under the Sinai covenant, but he is under the broken covenant of works, where the moral law is written on the heart (Rom. 2:14–15). The king of Tyre's self-deifying hubris violates natural law; it breaks God's covenant with creation.

Isaiah 24:5. All this evidence from Genesis 2–3, however, does not stand alone. Several other passages in God's holy Word support the covenantal nature of Genesis 2–3. First, there is Isaiah 24:5. Here God is denouncing in judgment the inhabitants of the earth for having transgressed the law and statutes; they broke the everlasting covenant. The laws in view in this passage are creational, and all humanity remains under them. And the result of mankind's unrighteousness is that the earth mourns and withers. The earth suffers under the curse via Genesis 3.

Earth's inhabitants rebelled against God's law, which Isaiah equates with breaking the everlasting covenant. This everlasting covenant is a covenant all mankind is under, and it is termed everlasting for its enduring character. Even though, after the fall, no one is able to meet the condition of perfect obedience, all people are under the covenant of works as they still owe God obedience and are subject to the curse and punishment of the original covenant. For all mankind to be under such a covenant, it must be the same covenant God made with Adam as the father of all humanity. Isaiah, then, assumes the covenant of works in order to apply it to all fallen humanity.

Hosea 6:7. This passage reflects the covenant with Adam by saying, "But like Adam they transgressed the covenant; there they dealt faithlessly with me." The prophet here is actually making a play off of Adam. He is pointing to two entities named Adam: the first man

Adam, and a town named Adam. Both referents characterize the severe nature of Israel's sin. Hosea's allusion to the person of Adam invokes similarity. Like Israel, Adam broke the Lord's covenant by failing to obey and suffered the curses of the covenant. Thus, the Mosaic covenant resembles the covenant made with Adam in that God demanded perfect obedience to obtain life in the land/garden as God's people. Like Adam, Israel failed to obey and so failed to have life as God's people. Israel's constant failure to keep the covenant similar to Adam's shows that post-fall man cannot earn life by keeping the law. Once more, the prophet's interpretation of Genesis 2–3 peeks through his prophecy, and it reveals that Adam was in covenant with God.[13]

Romans 5:12–19 and 1 Corinthians 15:21–22. In both of these passages, the apostle Paul compares Adam and Christ as a matching pair. The apostle's point about Christ in Romans 5:19–21 and 1 Corinthians 15:21–22 is dependent on the similarities he draws between Adam and Christ. Without a doubt Paul highlights differences between them, which are also drastically crucial, but the differences are meaningless without the more baseline similarities. Paul, therefore, calls Adam a type of the one who was to come, namely Jesus Christ (Rom. 5:14). By *type* here, Paul means God made Adam to be a model or example of Christ to come. A type is like this: On your tenth birthday, your dad promises you he will give you a candy-apple-red Porsche when you graduate from college, and he gives you an exact scale-model replica of the Porsche as a reminder of his promise. Sure, there are all kinds of differences between the model and the real car, but the reason your dad gives you the model is so that you have an idea what the real one is going to be like. So at night, you sit on your bed looking at the model car, dreaming of the real thing. Well, Adam is the model, and Christ is the reality.

As we discussed in chapter 1, Christ was in covenant with God the Father where he had to obey perfectly to earn life for his people, as it says in Romans 5:19, "By the one man's obedience the many will be made righteous." Christ is the covenant representative of his people

---

13. For an excellent treatment of Hosea 6:7, see See Byron G. Curtis, "Hosea 6:7 and Covenant-Breaking like/at Adam," in *The Law is not of Faith* (ed. Bryan D. Estelle, J. V. Fesko, and David VanDrunen; New Jersey: P&R, 2009), 170–209.

so that his free gift of righteousness leads to eternal life for those in Christ. If this is true of Christ, then it is true of Adam. Adam was the covenant representative of humanity, so that by his sin, sin came into the world and death through sin. The covenant relationship between the covenant heads and God are analogous. Likewise, the means whereby the promise and curse came are the same, namely obedience or the lack thereof. Works determined the outcome. Adam's disobedience brought death to all, and Christ's obedience bring life to all who believe in him (1 Cor. 15:21–22). This parallel between Adam and Christ is so balanced and important for Paul that he can even call Jesus Christ the last Adam in 1 Corinthians 15:45. The covenant of works is in parallel to the covenant of redemption. Paul's exegesis of Adam cements our conscience to believe the biblical doctrine of the covenant of works.

Why Is This Doctrine Important for the Christian Life?

The biblical evidence strongly builds the doctrinal edifice of the covenant of works. But how does the covenant of works form the pillars of the gospel bridge? Why is this doctrine important? What are some of its ramifications? Well, Adam's failure in the covenant of works directly impacts our present condition. His fall brought death to all men and resulted in this creation being cursed. Because Adam sinned, his guilt was imputed to us and we inherited his corrupt nature. The broken nature of the covenant of works demonstrates that we cannot keep God's law to earn life everlasting. In Adam's fall, we died. Sin came to all, and with sin its curse, namely death.

Additionally, the covenant of works reveals the standard of God's justice. In the garden, God assigned the price of everlasting life with him as perfect obedience to his law. After the fall, this does not change. God's law did not change, and neither did his requirement for life. The covenant of works reveals that heaven must be earned. God's justice means he cannot merely give away eternal life. Life must be earned by perfect righteousness according to the law.

Finally, the covenant of works made with the first Adam sheds light on the work of the last Adam. To deny or redefine the covenant of works is to do the same to the work of Christ. Thus, Christ comes as the last Adam, as our representative. What he earns comes to us.

Where Adam failed to earn life for his descendants, Christ succeeds by fulfilling all righteousness and so meriting heaven for himself and his people. Heaven must be earned before it can be given as a gift. Christ earned heaven and then gives it to us as a free gift through faith.

The covenant of works, then, is the necessary background and foundation for the doctrine of justification. Adam sinned, and his sin was imputed to us. But Christ, as the last Adam, took our sin upon himself and then earned heaven by his righteousness, so that his righteousness could be imputed to us. Christ, who had no sin, became sin for us so that we might become the righteousness of God in him. Our salvation is all of free grace because Christ met the terms of God's justice for us. This is love. When we were enemies deserving the eternal pains of hell, Christ died for us so that we might become co-heirs of heaven with him. In Christ, God's justice and mercy kiss. God the Father saves us, not by denying his own holy justice, but by satisfying its claims in the sending of his Son to die. The covenant of works forms the sturdy pillars of the gospel bridge so that when the eyes of our hearts behold them, God increases our assurance.

Questions for Further Reflection

1. Who were the parties of the original covenant of works? *Adam, God*
2. Was there a mediator of the covenant of works? *No one then. After the fall? Christ*
3. What in Genesis 2–3 makes clear that Adam's relationship to God is a covenant? *reward & punishment*
4. How does the covenant of works shed light on the work of Christ, and how does this strengthen your assurance? *He earned eternal life for us*
5. How do the two trees of Genesis 2–3 symbolize the terms and sanctions of the covenant of works? *Tree of life = eternal life. Tree of good & evil = death*
6. What does Adam's role as a priest of the paradise-sanctuary have to do with the covenant of works? *Priest is to keep and serve in the sanctuary.*

I Will Be Your God:
THE COVENANT OF GRACE

The twentieth-century author and Oxford professor J. R. R. Tolkien once coined a term for stories with plots that turned from disaster to hope through extraordinary events. He called this type of story a "eucatastrophe."[1] He took the word *catastrophe* to describe a devastating and horrific situation and attached the Greek prefix *eu*, which essentially means *good*. So, a plot that appears to unravel into utter hopelessness for the main characters but then suddenly turns for their good in the end is a eucatastrophe. Tolkien's epic trilogy *Lord of the Rings* is such a story. Although the darkness of the evil lord Sauron spreads across Middle Earth, and his victory appears certain, he is suddenly defeated by the modest little hobbit Frodo who, though on a mission to destroy the one ring to which Sauron's power is tied, sadly gave in to temptation and claimed the ring for himself. "I choose not now to do what I came to do," said Frodo. "I will not do this deed. The Ring is mine!" Though all hope seemed to be lost, destruction finally came to the ring (thanks to Gollum's uncontrollable lusts) and to Sauron. Consequently, Middle Earth was saved.

Similarly, we can call Genesis 1–3 a eucatastrophe. Describing factual and historical events, the opening chapters of Genesis reach their climax when the offended Lord of the covenant comes to judge his servant Adam for his rebellion in the covenant of works.

---

1. See his 1947 essay, "On Fairy Stories" in J.R.R. Tolkien, *The Tolkien Reader* (New York: Ballantine, 1966).

Yet, surprisingly, the Lord promises to send a second Adam who would fulfill the work the first Adam failed to do and thus bring his people to the Tree of Life and the blessed state for which they were created. Thus into the darkness and despair of Adam's catastrophe came a shining beam of hope from God's promise. Although he and his wife tried to make a covenant with the devil and were consequently expelled from the garden, he received a surprising promise that suddenly turned his circumstances for the better and guaranteed victory. Because God is just, he had to judge Adam and the human race for their sin. But in his grace he also promised to separate and put enmity between the offspring of the woman and the offspring of Satan. He promised to bring from the woman's offspring One who would conquer the Serpent and crush his head.

This happens in Genesis 3:15, which contains the *protevangelium*, the very first announcement of the gospel and the redemption that would be accomplished by Christ. Since Adam broke the first covenant, the covenant of works, God made a second covenant, the covenant of grace.

What Is the Covenant of Grace?

The covenant of grace is the one covenant through which all believers are saved. It began in Genesis 3:15 with God's promise to send a Savior and runs throughout redemptive history until Christ's second coming. Although it has been administered differently during different epochs of redemptive history, its substance remains the same in all periods. In other words, in both the Old Testament and New Testament the way in which God saves sinners is always the same: by his grace alone, through faith alone, because of Christ alone. Christ is the one Mediator of the one covenant of grace that unifies the one people of God in all periods of redemptive history, as shown in figure 1 below.

Figure 1. Timeline of the Covenant of Grace

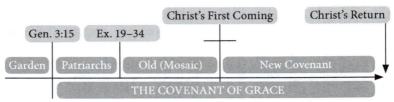

The covenant of grace was administered by type and shadow (that is, symbolic pictures of the reality) during the times of the patriarchs (that is, <u>Seth, Noah, Abraham, Isaac, and Jacob</u>) and of the nation Israel, as believers put their trust in God's promise to send the Messiah. It is administered in more fullness, however, in the new covenant, as believers put their trust in the Messiah who lived, died, and was raised again from the dead.

The covenant of grace is the historical outworking of God's eternal plan of salvation in the covenant of redemption. As we learned in chapter 1, the covenant of redemption was made in eternity among the persons of the Trinity and fulfilled in time through Christ's active obedience and atoning death. It was for Christ a covenant of works. Just as there was a covenant of works with the first Adam, there was also a covenant of works with the second Adam, Christ. <u>His obedience under this covenant is the foundation of the gospel and the covenant of grace. The covenant of grace is essentially the application to sinners of the benefits earned by Christ through his fulfillment of the covenant of redemption.</u> In this covenant, because of Christ's obedience, God brings his people into communion with himself and promises them, "I will be your God, and you will be my people." His promise is not on the basis of *their* obedience, but on the basis of *Christ's* obedience. It was works for Christ so that it is grace for us. "For as by the one man's disobedience the many were made sinners, so also by the one man's obedience the many will be made righteous" (Rom. 5:19).

<u>Like the covenant of works, the covenant of grace is made between God and humans. One of the chief differences between these two covenants, however, is that the latter has a Mediator between God and his covenant partners, whereas the former does not.</u> Christ is that Mediator (1 Tim. 2:5). This makes the nature of these covenants very different from one another. As was shown in chapter 2, the covenant of works is based on law and requires perfect, personal obedience. Its condition is, "Do this and you will live" (cf. Lev. 18:5; Gal. 3:12). <u>The covenant of grace, on the other hand, is based on God's promise to save sinners.</u> Its condition is, "Believe in the Lord Jesus Christ, and you will be saved" (Acts 16:31; cf. Rom. 10:6–13; Gal. 2:16). In the covenant of grace, God pronounces sinners justified and righteous

on the basis of the righteousness of Christ imputed to them and received through faith alone. Figure 2 shows the distinction between the covenants of works and grace.

Figure 2. The Distinction Between the Covenants of Works and Grace

	COVENANT OF WORKS	COVENANT OF GRACE
Parties	God and Adam	God and believers and their children
Time made	Eden	First promised in Genesis 3:15
Condition	Perfect obedience	Faith in Christ, the One who was perfectly obedient
Mediator	None	Christ
Promise	Glorified life	Justification and glorified life

Contrary to the teachings of classical Dispensationalism, the Bible does not teach two plans of salvation for two peoples of God (that is, Israel and the church), but rather *one* plan of salvation for *one* people of God throughout redemptive history. God's one plan of salvation is in the historical outworking of the covenant of grace.

Thus, we may define the covenant of grace as *the covenant between God and believers with their children, in which he promises salvation through faith in Christ, who merited their salvation by his obedience in the covenant of redemption.*

What Does the Bible Teach?

Like the phrases "covenant of redemption" and "covenant of works," the phrase "covenant of grace" does not appear in Scripture. Nevertheless, Scripture clearly teaches this doctrine as the historical arrangement for God's grace mediated to his people through the Lord Jesus Christ.

Genesis 3:15–24. While the covenant of grace is more fully revealed in Genesis 12, 15, and 17 with God's covenant to Abraham, which is then fulfilled in two great stages, the old (Mosaic) and new covenants, its "mother" or "seed" promise is in the *protevangelium* of Genesis 3:15. As Meredith Kline put it, "The Genesis 3 narrative of the judgment that terminated the original covenantal order in Eden is, therefore, at the same time the record of the inauguration of the new redemptive order of the Covenant of Grace."[2] This becomes clear when we examine four features of God's promise in this text: first, his termination of the sinful covenant between Satan and the woman; second, his placing enmity between the Serpent's offspring and the woman's offspring; third, his promise of a Messiah who will judge the Serpent; and fourth, Adam's response to this promise.

First, God terminated the sinful covenant between Satan and the woman. The Lord says to the Serpent, "I will put enmity between you and the woman." God declares that he will not allow the devil to remain in covenant with the man and the woman, which is essentially what happened in the fall. In his tempting of the woman (Gen. 3:1–6), the Serpent casts doubt on God's goodness and truthfulness by challenging the covenant stipulations. "Did God actually say, 'You shall not eat of any tree in the garden?'... You will not surely die." He attempts to derail God's kingdom plan to bring his image-bearers to glory. He sees that God made Adam his servant/vassal in the covenant of works, so he tries to forestall the coming of the eternal blessings by getting Adam barred from the Tree of Life. He knows that if he can get Adam to violate the covenant of works, then God (being just by nature) must judge him according to the stipulations he made. At first, the Serpent's scheme seems to work. He manages to persuade the woman (and consequently Adam) to disbelieve God and enter into league with himself. Yet, after Adam's fall, God does not permit that sinful relationship to continue. He puts enmity between the Serpent and the woman. Reconciliation between God and humans would be made through a new covenant, since the original covenant of works was violated and broken. But the devil did not realize that God had planned to send a second Adam who would bring his kingdom project to completion.

---

2. Meredith Kline, *Kingdom Prologue: Genesis Foundations for a Covenantal Worldview* (Overland Park, KS: Two Age Press, 2000), 143.

Second, the Lord puts enmity between the Serpent's offspring and the woman's offspring. He promises to form a community of people for himself whom he will set apart from the offspring of the devil and one day rescue from the latter's fierce hostility. The Hebrew word for *offspring* (or *seed*) dominates the book of Genesis, appearing at least thirty-seven times in chapters 12–50.³ This indicates God's faithfulness to his promise to form a community of believers and their children called out from the world and the offspring of the devil. This community can be traced throughout redemptive history and into the new covenant, not by bloodline, but by those who believe in God's promise. As Paul says to Gentile Christians in Galatians 3:29: "And if you are Christ's, then you are Abraham's offspring, heirs according to the promise." Thus, Genesis 3:15 reveals God's first formation of his church.

Third, the Lord promised a Messiah who would judge the Serpent, doing the work the first Adam failed to accomplish: "He shall bruise your head, and you shall bruise his heel." The Lord shifts from the collective offspring to a singular offspring. Like the English word *offspring*, the Hebrew word can refer to one's children (Gen. 4:25; 15:3), a distant descendant, or a large group of descendants. Here in Genesis 3:15, we encounter both the singular and collective senses of this word, which tells us that the Lord would not only form a people from the woman and make them his holy covenant community but he would also from the woman bring a Champion-Offspring who would defeat the Serpent.

That the first Adam failed in his responsibility to carry out judgment on the Serpent is further elucidated in verses 23–24, which tell us that the Lord relieved Adam of his priestly duty of protecting the holiness of the garden and gave it to the cherubim with the flaming sword. In Genesis 2:15 we are told that "the LORD God took the man and put him in the garden of Eden to work and keep it."⁴ In order to reach the goal of the Tree of Life, Adam was to remain obedient in these covenant responsibilities. He was not only to take care of the garden as a gardener but also protect it as a guardian. Eden was a

---

3. The Hebrew word for offspring/seed is *zerà*.
4. The Hebrew words for *work* and *keep* in Genesis 2:15 are the words *àbad* and *shamar* respectively.

holy temple and sanctuary to the Lord. Protecting it from defilement was part of his priestly responsibility to the Lord. Thus, he failed in the covenant of works even before he ate of the forbidden tree. He failed when he allowed his wife to enter into league with the devil. At that very point, he should have exercised his priestly authority and executed judgment on the Serpent. Consequently, "the LORD God sent him out from the garden of Eden to work ground from which he was taken. He drove out the man, and at the east of the garden of Eden he placed the cherubim and a flaming sword that turned every way to guard the way to the tree of life" (Gen. 3:23–24).[5] Fallen Adam would continue in his responsibility to "till" or "tend" the earth (now cursed and bearing thorns) as an everyday function for life. But his holy responsibility of "guarding" the garden was taken from him and given to the cherubim as he failed in his priestly duty to protect Eden from defilement. If God's elect were to reach the goal of the Tree of Life, God would need to send a new Adam to exercise judgment on the Serpent, which is precisely what he promises in Genesis 3:15: "He will bruise your head."

God's promise of a Champion seed is central to the unfolding drama of redemptive history. Throughout the Old Testament, the people of God look forward to their Messiah who will vanquish Satan and give them victory over his offspring. The Bible repeats this champion concept in stories like David and Goliath (1 Sam. 17). In this famous account, the battle between the Israelites and the Philistines comes down to these two champions, each of whom represents his people as a federal head. If David defeats Goliath, the Philistines will become slaves to Israel, but the opposite will result if Goliath defeats David. As David defeats Goliath (even removing his head!), he foreshadows his descendant Christ who would defeat Satan and obtain victory for his people.

This is why when Christ began his earthly ministry he was "led up by the Spirit into the wilderness to be tempted by the devil" (Matt. 4:1). Like the first Adam, Jesus was also tempted by the devil to enter into covenant with him (Matt. 4:1–11). But unlike the first Adam, Jesus did not succumb to those temptations; instead, he remained

---

5. The same Hebrew words for *work* and *guard* are used in Genesis 3:23–24 as in Genesis 2:15, namely, *'abad* and *shamar*.

faithful and obedient in his covenant with the Father. He even rebuked the devil and drove him away with judicial directive: "Be gone, Satan! For it is written, 'You shall worship the Lord your God and him only shall you serve" (Matt. 4:10). Unlike the first Adam, this Champion-Offspring passed his probationary test.

But Christ's victory over Satan also required him to undergo the horrors of the cross. As the Lord promised in Genesis 3:15, "He shall bruise your head, and you shall bruise his heel." For the Champion-Offspring to deliver his people from the power of death, he would need to taste death himself. As Hebrews tells us: "Since therefore the children share in flesh and blood, he himself likewise partook of the same things, that through death he might destroy the one who has the power of death, that is, the devil, and deliver all those who through fear of death were subject to lifelong slavery. For surely it is not angels that he helps, but he helps the offspring of Abraham." (Heb. 2:14–16). Our Champion not only came as the second Adam to fulfill all righteousness in his actively obedient life but he also came as the suffering Servant, to suffer the curse to which the woman's offspring were liable. Without suffering the wrath of God against their sins, Christ could not have made atonement for his people nor exercised redemptive judgment against Satan, as was promised in Genesis 3:15. It is through his obedient life and atoning death, then, that Christ trampled the head of the Serpent.

The fourth feature we observe from this passage is Adam's response of faith in God's promise, as well as God's clothing of Adam and Eve with the garments of a slain animal. Notice that Eve's name is not given until *after* God's promise in Genesis 3:15. Up to this point, she is known only as "the woman," because she was taken out of the man (see Gen. 2:23).[6] In 3:20, however, we are told, "The man called his wife's name Eve, because she was the mother of all living." Where did that idea come from? It came from God's promise to reverse the curse of death on humans through the Champion-Offspring of the covenant of grace. Adam and Eve believed this promise with true faith (demonstrated in Adam's naming of Eve), and they were justified. God then removed the useless garments they

---

6. The similarity between the words *woman* and *man* is also seen in the Hebrew of Gen. 2–3: the word for *woman* is *'ishah,* and the word for *man* is *'ish.*

made of fig leaves in an attempt to cover their shame (which did not provide any protection against God's holiness and righteousness) and instead clothed them with the skins of an animal that had to suffer death. Their physical nakedness was not intrinsically evil but was a symbol of their spiritual nakedness. The very fact that they were trying to run away from God showed that Adam had broken the covenant of works, and their own consciences were testifying against them. Nevertheless, because they believed in his promise, he provided garments for them and clothed them so that they would no longer be guilty and ashamed.

Genesis 3:15 is not only a prophecy of the coming Christ but the Mother Promise of the whole covenant of grace from which the rest of the Scriptures unfold.

Genesis 1–11. These chapters reveal God's faithfulness in maintaining the offspring of the woman in the birth of Seth (Gen. 4), Adam's descendants leading to Noah (Gen. 5), the protection of Noah's line in the great flood (Gen. 6–9), Noah's descendants leading to Shem (Gen. 10), and Shem's descendants leading to Abraham (Gen. 11). The first eleven chapters of Genesis are ancient history and given to us in a broad, overview fashion. Once we get to chapter 12, though, Abraham enters the scene and the speed of the camera slows down. God calls him out of Ur and establishes his covenant of grace with him. The genealogies of Genesis 5 and 11 are the link between the Mother Promise of Genesis 3:15 and Abraham.

This link is critical to the covenant of grace, for Genesis 12–17 makes known the Abrahamic covenant, which, as we will see in chapter 5, is God's primary revelation of his covenant of grace. While God first promises the covenant of grace in Genesis 3:15, he expands on that promise in his covenant with Abraham, promising him an offspring and a land. These promises are fulfilled in two stages: first in the nation Israel (offspring) and Canaan (land) during the old (Mosaic) covenant, and second in the church of Christ (offspring) and the new heavens and new earth (land) during the new covenant. The Abrahamic covenant has a strong continuity with its fulfillment in the new covenant, thus showing us the unity of the one covenant of grace. As Horton says, it "establishes the basis for the everlasting inheritance of the heavenly Jerusalem," while the Mosaic covenant (which came four hundred years later) "establishes the terms of the temporal inheritance of the earthly Jerusalem" as a picture pointing forward to the reign of God in Christ.[7]

The Covenant Formula Echoed in Redemptive History. The essence of the covenant of grace is summarized in God's promise: "I will be your God, and you shall be my people." This promise echoes throughout redemptive history. God made this promise to Abraham when he ordained the covenant sign of circumcision (Gen. 17:7). Over four hundred years later, God made this same promise to Abraham's biological descendants when he brought them out of slavery in Egypt (Ex. 6:7). He made it to them again as he prescribed the blessings they would inherit for their obedience to the Sinai covenant (Lev. 26:11–12). Much later in Israel's history, after centuries of disobedience to the Sinai covenant, God made this promise again, this time in connection to his promise of a new covenant (Jer. 31:33; cf. Ezek. 34:23–24; 37:26–27). This same promise is also found in the New Testament as Paul applies it to believers, both Jew and Gentile (2 Cor. 6:16). Finally, we hear this promise in the closing chapters of Revelation, which record John's vision of a new heaven and new earth in the future (Rev. 21:2–3). Thus, God's promise in the one covenant of grace runs from Genesis to Revelation, revealing its continuity and the unifying nature of redemptive history.

What Does Reformed Theology Teach?

At the time of the Protestant Reformation, the Reformers developed this distinction between the covenants of works and grace in order to defend the gospel against the teachings of the medieval church. Rome generally held that justification is not a one-time forensic (legal) act in which Christ's obedience and righteousness are imputed (credited to one's account) to the believer, but a gradual process of moral change in the believer's life, wrought by infused (imparted) grace. This teaching arose from the belief that God can only declare righteous those people who truly are righteous.[8]

---

7. Horton, *God of Promise*, 105.

8. This ontological understanding of justification arose in large part from the distinction made by late medieval scholastic theologians between congruent merit (*meritum de congruo*) and condign merit (*meritum de condign*). The former was a

The Roman Catholic Church officially adopted this teaching at the Council of Trent (1545–65), thus confusing the law with the gospel, and the doctrines of justification and sanctification.[9] In response to this, the Reformers of the sixteenth and seventeenth centuries turned to covenant theology, and particularly the sharp distinction between the covenants of works and grace. They did this to show how the Bible clearly distinguishes between law and gospel, and that the way of salvation in both the old covenant and new covenant is the same: by grace alone (*sola gratia*), through faith alone (*sola fide*), in Christ alone (*solus Christus*), mediated in one unifying covenant of grace.

As we pointed out in chapter 2, Ursinus and Olevianus, the writers of the Heidelberg Catechism, taught this bi-covenantal distinction of works and grace. So did Reformed theologians across Europe, such as the Scotsman Robert Rollock (1555–98), the Englishman William Perkins (1558–1602), the German Amandus Polanus (1561–1610), and the Swiss Johannes Wollebius (1586–1629), just to name a few. In the 1640s, the Westminster Assembly officially codified this distinction in its confession and catechisms. WCF chapter 7, for example, reads in part:

> 2. The first covenant made with man was a covenant of works, wherein life was promised to Adam, and in him to his posterity, on condition of perfect and personal obedience.
>
> 3. Man by his fall having made himself incapable of life by that covenant, the Lord was pleased to make a second, commonly called the covenant of grace; wherein He freely offereth unto sinners life and salvation by Jesus Christ, requiring of them faith in Him that they may be saved, and promising to give unto

---

half-merit, not truly deserving of God's grace; it received grace proportionate to and congruent with a believer's good works on the basis of divine generosity. The latter, on the other hand, was a full merit, truly deserving of God's grace. Connected to this was the teaching of the Franciscan Order that God's covenant was essentially, "To those who do what is in them, God will not deny grace" (*facientibus quod in se est, Deus non denegat gratiam*). The Reformers and their orthodox heirs, on the other hand, rejected the medieval notion of congruent merit and instead embraced a doctrine of imputed condign merit—merit that the first Adam failed to achieve but that the second Adam attained through his active obedience—to the sinner who received it through faith alone.

9. See, for example, Council of Trent, session 6, chapter 7, and session 6, canons 10–12, and 24.

all those that are ordained unto life His Holy Spirit, to make them willing and able to believe.

The Westminster Larger Catechism (WLC) expresses this distinction even more succinctly:

> Q.30. Doth God leave all mankind to perish in the estate of sin and misery?
>
> A. God doth not leave all men to perish in the estate of sin and misery, into which they fell by the breach of the first covenant, commonly called the Covenant of Works; but of his mere love and mercy delivereth his elect out of it, and bringeth them into an estate of salvation by the second covenant, commonly called the Covenant of Grace.

It then goes on to point out faith as the sole condition of the covenant of grace:

> Q.32. How is the grace of God manifested in the second covenant?
>
> A. The grace of God is manifested in the second covenant, in that he freely provideth and offereth to sinners a Mediator, and life and salvation by him; and requiring faith as the condition to interest them in him, promiseth and giveth his Holy Spirit to all his elect, to work in them that faith, with all other saving graces; and to enable them unto all holy obedience, as the evidence of the truth of their faith and thankfulness to God, and as the way which he hath appointed them to salvation.

As the answer above makes clear, even the condition of faith is a gift (Eph 2:8-9), which, along with every redemptive benefit given to the believer, was earned for us by Christ's merits alone.

Like the Heidelberg Catechism (HC Q.19) and the Belgic Confession (BC Article 17), the WCF and WLC teach that the covenant of grace began at the *protevangelium* of Genesis 3:15 and runs throughout redemptive history until the consummation (see WCF 7.5-6 and WLC 33-34). It was administered differently under different epochs, but its substance is the same in every period after Adam's fall. This is because it has the same Mediator.

Moreover, the Reformed confessions teach that the covenant of grace was made with believers *and their children,* as this is God's design in both the Old Testament and New Testament (HC Q.74; BC 34; WCF 28.4; WLC 166). In the historical administration of the covenant of grace, membership in the visible covenant community or the church is not limited to the elect. Until the consummation, the covenant of grace contains both Jacobs and Esaus, that is to say, both those who believe God's covenant promise with true faith and those who reject it. Nevertheless, the children of believers are included into this visible covenant community and distinguished from the children of unbelievers. We will explore this further in chapter 5 on the Abrahamic covenant.

Why Is This Doctrine Important for the Christian Life?

The covenant of grace is important for the Christian life for several reasons. First, it tells us that we are not under a covenant of works and therefore do not relate to God on the basis of our own law-keeping. In the covenant of grace, God promises to accept us as righteous by virtue of the righteousness of his Son, the second Adam. In other words, God's covenant of grace draws attention to the doctrine of justification by faith alone. Whereas the covenant of works (law) says, "Do this and you will live," the covenant of grace (gospel) says, "Christ did it for you." This allows us to go through life on the solid foundation that God receives us because of Christ. There is no greater contributing factor to our joy and comfort as Christians than the reality that God accepts us *in spite* of the fact that we still struggle with sin and disobedience. Knowing that God loves us on account of Christ protects us from the rollercoaster of our own conscience and emotions. With its emphasis on the person and work of Christ, the covenant of grace tells us that we are not under a covenant of works.

Second, the covenant of grace teaches us that the whole Bible is about one thing: God redeeming a people for himself through Jesus Christ. As Edmund Clowney said, "It is possible to know Bible stories, yet miss *the* Bible story."

> The Bible is much more than William How stated: 'a golden casket where gems of truth are stored.' It is more than a bewildering collection of oracles, proverbs, poems, architectural directions,

annals, and prophecies. The Bible has a story line. It traces an unfolding drama. The story follows the history of Israel, but it does not begin there, nor does it contain what you would expect in a national history. The narrative does not pay tribute to Israel. Rather, it regularly condemns Israel and justifies God's severest judgments. The story is God's story. It describes His work to rescue rebels from their folly, guilt, and ruin.[10]

The covenant of grace tells God's story of redemption; it traces the unfolding drama from Genesis to Revelation. It shows us that the Bible is actually *one* book with *one* story, told on the stage of real human history. Without seeing the big picture that the covenant of grace provides, we will be tempted to think of the Bible as being little more than a manual for ethical behavior or self-improvement. We will tend to think of the Bible as a compilation of stories with a moral point, sort of like Aesop's fables, or as a prophecy handbook that must be deciphered by current events. The covenant of grace, however, guards us from these pitfalls by highlighting the point and plotline of Scripture. It unifies the Scriptures and sets every story in the context of the larger story about Christ, who was promised in Genesis 3:15, came in the fullness of time, and will return again. Few things are more important for us to understand as we read God's Word and seek to know him more.

Third, the covenant of grace reminds us that we are pilgrims in this age, and the end of the story is yet to come. As Christians, we sometimes assume that our lives should be free from the trouble and messiness of this world. We tend to think that because we are Christians we should have normal lives immune, or at least less susceptible, to suffering and letdown. But the truth is that, until the consummation, there is no such thing as "normal life." There is a scene in the movie *Tombstone* that illustrates this rather well. Near the end of the film, when Wyatt Earp goes to see his friend Doc Holliday as he lies on his deathbed, Doc tells Wyatt how he was in love once, but the woman he loved joined a convent. "She was all I ever wanted," he said. He then asked his friend, "What did you want out of life, Wyatt?" With a cynical tone that came from

---

10. Edmund Clowney, *The Unfolding Mystery: Discovering Christ in the Old Testament* (Phillipsburg: P & R, 1988), 11.

years of difficulty and heartbreak, Wyatt responded, "Just to live a normal life." Rather surprised, Doc answered back, "There is no normal life, Wyatt. There's just life." Most people who saw the film could identify with that line, for there is no normal life free from complications; there is just life with its messiness and ups and downs. Normal life ended in Genesis 3 with the fall and disobedience of our first parents. <u>The covenant of grace, however, with its long saga of fallible sinner-saints who trusted in God's promise, tells us about pilgrim life</u>. It does not promise us that our lives in this fallen world will be protected from complications any more than our neighbor, but it does promise us that a glorious end awaits us. <u>The covenant of grace points us to the heavenly goal that the first Adam never reached</u>, <u>but that the second Adam has secured for us</u>. It tells us that this life is temporary, and the best is yet to come.

Questions for Further Reflection

1. What is the difference between the covenant of works and the covenant of grace? *[handwritten: earn one's own righteousness / Christ earned righteousness for us]*
2. What were God's promises in Genesis 3:15? *[handwritten: To send a savior; To break the serpent's relationship w/ Eve; to have a church]*
3. With whom is the covenant of grace made? *[handwritten: The elect]*
4. How does the covenant of grace highlight the person and work of Christ? Why is this important for the Christian life? *[handwritten: Prays after to justification by faith alone / (p. 69)]*
5. How does the covenant of grace unify the whole Bible? Why is this important for the way that we read the Scriptures? *[handwritten: (a) It teaches us that the Bible is about one thing: God redeeming a people for himself through Jesus Christ. (b) So we don't read the Bible as a manual of "do's" and "don'ts" (c) by setting every story in the context of the larger story about Christ]*

Promise in the Clouds:
THE COMMON GRACE COVENANT

As Christians, we regularly feel the anti-Christian character of American and Western European society. Despite such impressions, though, there is no missing the sense of guilt and judgment in popular culture. It seems that every year some new movie comes to the box office dramatizing the fight for survival of the last few humans after some cataclysmic disaster. Whether the worldwide undoing is a nuclear holocaust, alien invasion, or environmental abuse, the apocalyptic tones remain consistent. Each film contains some sort of Noah figure who survives to give the human race a new beginning. Yet, no matter how far-fetched the movies get, their presence and popularity seem to reflect humanity's sense of guilt and fear that the world will one day crumble in destruction. Whether the cataclysm is man-made or not, there is a common sentiment that this world cannot continue the way it is; humanity needs a fresh start.

The Bible, however, does not leave us in doubt about these things. First of all, our Lord Jesus has promised to destroy the world once more in his second coming. Yet the destruction he will bring will result in the new heavens and new earth, where his people will dwell with him forever in glory. For those in Christ, the final day of the Lord is a day we do not have to fear. Rather, we look forward to it with eager expectation for the redemption of the body. Second, God has also promised that there would be no more Noah figures. The Lord of heaven and earth will not destroy the world again by water, requiring another Noah. No matter how many scary and realistic doomsday prophecies our culture dishes up, God's promise stands. His rainbow still shines after the rain.

The significance of the Lord's promise, however, extends much further than anything portrayed in modern movies. At the end of God's multi-colored bow rests a theological pot of gold. The Lord's promise not to destroy the world is a covenant, with an integral place in Reformed theology. The Noahic covenant is the covenant of common grace, the realm of our everyday lives under the sun. Its theological significance extends in several directions. It broadcasts how God governs this world and its goodness; it discloses some of man's obligations and roles in the world; and it even points us to Christ. The Noahic covenant is crucial to a biblical understanding of the world and is a necessary part of covenant theology.

What Is the Common Grace Covenant?

In discussions of Reformed covenant theology, the Noahic covenant tends to be like salt at the dinner table. It is not mentioned in the menu and sometimes is not passed around the table, but it is always present, for without it the whole dinner suffers. Often consideration of the Noahic covenant is missing in Reformed discussions because it is a non-redemptive covenant. God's promise in this covenant is not for salvation. Most Reformed works on covenant theology focus on God's work of redemption, but God does not promise redemption for his people in the Noahic covenant. Rather, he promises to sustain the natural order. This does not make it insubstantial, though, nor does it mean that it does not touch upon our salvation. In fact, the reason for God's promise not to destroy is in service of his redemptive plans. Hence, any family picture of covenant theology is incomplete without the Noahic.

To begin, it is necessary to define common grace. *Common grace is God's undeserved kindness to all people, no matter what their religious status.* This grace of God is labeled *common*, in contrast to his *special* grace. God's special grace is his saving grace. It is his saving favor on his special people that results in their salvation. The blessings of special grace are those like regeneration, justification, and adoption (Rom. 8:28–30). God does not give these blessings to the unregenerate of the world. They are special because they are given only to those chosen in Christ before the foundation of the world. The blessings of common grace, however, are common to both regenerate and unregenerate, both the church and the world.

Common refers, then, to what is held in common between the saved and the unsaved. Common grace blessings include sunshine, rain, food, and possessions (Matt. 5:45; Acts 14:17), wisdom or skill in crafts, trades, and learning (Dan. 1:4–5; 1 Kings 5:6; Prov. 30:1; 31:1), family, and friends. All these are blessings Christians receive along with non-Christians, and they are truly undeserved for us all, since we all deserve the curse of God's wrath due to our sin. They are common graces from God, and the Noahic covenant gives God's covenantal foundation for them.

The Noahic covenant can be defined as *God's covenant of common grace with the earth, despite mankind's depravity, to sustain its order until the consummation.*

What Does the Bible Teach?

Genesis 8:20–9:17. The portion of Scripture that presents the Noahic covenant is mainly contained within one passage, Genesis 8:20–9:17, though many more texts shed light on this covenant. The Genesis passage will preoccupy the majority of our discussion, as it is the actual statement of the covenant. The flood account closes up in Genesis 8:15–19 with God commanding Noah and all the animals to leave the ark in order to fill the earth. Verses 20–22 then form a bridge between the flood account and the covenant confirmation. Noah, as God's righteous servant, builds an altar and offers sacrifices to the Lord out of gratitude for the Lord bringing him safely through the flood judgment. At the smell of Noah's sacrifice, God says in his heart, "I will never again curse the ground because of man, for the intention of man's heart is evil from his youth. Neither will I ever again strike down every living creature as I have done. While the earth remains, seedtime and harvest, cold and heat, summer and winter, day and night, shall not cease" (verses 21–22).

Several things are noteworthy about God's statement. *First, it makes a promise with two prongs.* The first prong is that God will not destroy the earth because of man. God is vowing not to do something.

He will not judge the whole earth with water again. In the second prong, God promises to do something, which is consonant with the first prong: God promises to preserve the normal cycle of seasons. Animals will continue to live, and God will uphold the environment and climate necessary for life on earth. The change of seasons, the rain to make seeds grow until the harvest, and the passage of time in day and night will be sustained.

Second, God makes this promise despite humanity's depravity. The intention of humankind's heart is still evil from his youth. This ties back to Genesis 6:5, where the evil intention of man was the reason given for the flood judgment. Fallen man is no better after the flood than before. God grants them life under the sun even though they still deserve punishment. God keeping his promise is not dependent on man's performance, be it righteous or wicked.

Finally, God makes this promise "in his heart" (v.8:21). This statement was not heard by Noah. One could say it was only audible in heaven. This is important, for it creates another link between this statement and God's speech in 9:8–17. In 9:9, God says directly to Noah and his sons that he will establish "my covenant with you." Here this phrase "establish a covenant" refers to a previously-made covenant that is being continued and confirmed. The question of Genesis 9:9 is *which* covenant God is establishing. The answer is God's promise in 8:20–22. This is borne out by the equivalent content between God's covenant confirmation in 9:8–17 and his promise in 8:21–22. This link demonstrates how Scripture uses the idea of covenant. The Scriptural authors still consider a promise from God with no overt covenantal context to have a covenantal character. Moreover, this link reveals that 8:20–9:17 is a unit. Hence, the regulations of 9:1–7 belong to the Noahic covenant, which we will explore further below.

Parties of the Covenant. Having considered the link between 8:21 and 9:8–17, let us now parse the nature of this covenant. Covenants are agreements between different parties, so who are the parties of this covenant? The first party is clearly God. It is *his* promise and covenant, because he is the sovereign of the covenant. The second party, however, is multiple in character. God makes his covenant with Noah, his descendants, and the animals (livestock, birds, and every beast), as in verse 10. But God names the second party over and over in varying ways. In verse 12, the covenant is with you and every living creature, for future generations. Noah, then, represents all future humanity. Verse 13 lists God and the earth, and the parties continue to be listed: between me and you and every living creature (v. 15); between God and every living creature of all flesh (v. 16); between me and all flesh (v. 17).

It is unmistakable that this covenant is common, not limited to God's special people. It is God's covenant with the earth, every living animal on the earth and all humanity descended from Noah and his sons. God's promise is to sustain, uphold, and govern the earth with all human and animal creatures on it. This makes this covenant non-redemptive. The promise is not to save the second party from sin and its curse, but it is to preserve the natural order of the world so that life can continue to exist, the elect can come forth, and the full number can be redeemed.

Sign of the covenant. This covenant also has a sign of commonness. As we pointed out, God's various covenants with his people typically have visible and symbolic signs that help administer or maintain the covenant relationship. Covenant signs, though, are only given to those who are party to the covenant relationship. For example, the Abrahamic sign of circumcision is only for the covenant family, and the new covenant signs of baptism and the Lord's Supper are only for members of the church. Those outside the covenant community do not receive the sign. In distinction from these redemptive covenant administrations, the Noahic sign is public and part of the natural world. The rainbow sign shines out from the clouds for every man and beast to see. Every creature included in the second party is witness to the sign of the covenant.

This public sign has further significance in that it is symbolic. Signs are symbolic of a particular idea or meaning. So what does the rainbow symbolize? There are two scholarly interpretations of the rainbow, both of which are worthy of mention. First, the Hebrew word for *rainbow* can mean either *rainbow* or *bow,* as in *bow and arrow.* God calls it "my bow" in verse 13. In ancient iconography, victorious kings and gods are pictured coming back from war with their bows in a horizontal position (like a rainbow). Going into battle, the king/god has the bow vertical in hand, ready to shoot;

2 poss. meanings

but after battle it is horizontal, symbolizing the peace after war. The rainbow, then, could be symbolic of God's war bow that hangs in the sky, symbolic of peace. God will not destroy the world again; he is no longer hostile.

Second, the ancients understood the sky or firmament as a dome-shaped barrier that held back the waters above, as in Genesis 1:6–7. Hence, when God judged the world in the flood, he opened the windows of heaven, releasing the waters above (7:11). In fact, the Hebrew word for *flood* refers more specifically to these celestial waters. Thus, God's promise is that he will never wipe out all flesh by the waters of the flood. The rainbow then visually represents the dome-shaped firmament as shut.[1] The rainbow appears when it rains to show that the celestial waters will not be released.

The symbolic value of the rainbow could be either of these, or perhaps both. Either way, the effect of the symbol is clear. The rainbow reminds us that the floods will never come again. The beautiful arch points to God's promise that he will never judge the world by the waters of the flood. The firmament is shut; there is peace after the storm.

Terms of the Covenant. The sign of the Noahic covenant additionally reflects on the terms of this covenant. What are the terms of this covenant for its continuing validity? First, the sign identifies that it is a sign for God, so verse 16 says, "When the bow is in the clouds, I will see it and remember the everlasting covenant between God and every living creature of all flesh that is on the earth." God is the one who sees the sign and remembers his promise not to destroy but to sustain. The only term of the covenant is God keeping his promise. There are no terms for humanity or creation that they must meet for the covenant to continue. The covenant is a unilateral promise of God. It is by definition unbreakable. There are no conditional terms whereby the covenant can be broken.

This invincible nature of the covenant is reflected in Jeremiah 33:20–21a, "If you can break my covenant with the day and my covenant with the night, so that day and night will not come at

---

1. This connection between rainbow (*qešet*) and firmament (*rāqîʻa*) also shows up in Ezekiel 1:26–28, where cosmological description is taking place. See Laurence A. Turner, "The Rainbow as the Sign of the Covenant in Gen. IX 11–13," *VT* 43.1 (1993): 119–124.

their appointed time, then also my covenant with David my servant may be broken." The point of the Lord's comparison between his covenant with day and night and the Davidic is that they both are impossible to break; man can do nothing to invalidate them. Hence, God calls the Noahic covenant eternal. It is everlasting; it will last as long as the earth endures.

This aspect should strike us as outstanding. When we see the rainbow, we can know God is also gazing at it and remembering his everlasting covenant to uphold seedtime and harvest, day and night. With all the terror and grievous evil that humans have inflicted on each other, we may wonder why the globe keeps spinning. From our point of view, it is not an easy thing to keep this promise. But God is greater than we are, and his thoughts are higher than ours. He is a God who keeps his promises. *for man*

Regulations of the Covenant. The everlasting and unilateral nature of the Noahic covenant does not negate the fact that there are some obligations for mankind within this covenant. Indeed there are, but the continuance of the covenant does not depend on these obligations. As Meredith Kline points out, "Regulations governing mankind's conduct were included, but no commitments were exacted from man on which the continuance of the covenant itself or individual membership therein might be dependent."[2] The imposed regulations define how God governs his creation and how mankind should act in it. Yet the existence of the covenant is not dependent on man's fidelity to the regulations.

The regulations of the Noahic covenant are found in Genesis 9:1–7, three of which we will discuss here. First, God calls Noah and his sons to be fruitful and multiply (v. 1). *1st* This imperative reiterates what God told the animals in 8:17, and it parallels God's command in Genesis 1:28. Mankind and animals are to procreate. God sustains and orders this world through the increase of mankind and animals. Assumed in this command to be fruitful is marriage, of course. Therefore, marriage and procreation are a good and normal part of human society.

Second, God gives Noah all things for food (v. 3). *2nd* The distinction between clean and unclean animals in the ark is no longer in force.

---

2. Kline, *Kingdom Prologue*, 246.

Noah can eat of all animals and plants. God has given mankind a lordship over the animals. The good effect of this regulation is often overlooked. In fact, Paul has this regulation in mind when he says, "For everything created by God is good, and nothing is to be rejected if it is received with thanksgiving, for it is made holy by the word of God and prayer" (1 Tim. 4:4–5). Likewise, Paul states that it is "God, who richly provides us with everything to enjoy" (1 Tim. 6:17). God gave us these things to be enjoyed, for his glory. Our everyday meals, then, are about more than just nourishment, but about gratitude to God.

A corollary of this regulation is work. To eat of both animals and vegetation is to be a tiller of the soil and shepherd of herds. Cultivation and labor are the necessary means for taking all things for food. So God's food regulation displays his will that work is a good and necessary part of human life.

Third, God declares that whoever sheds the blood of man, by man his blood shall be shed (v. 6). This regulation not only reveals that murder is wrong but also that man has the right, even the duty, to punish with capital punishment such murderers. Indeed, the mention of man being made in the image of God is the basis for man being able to judge criminals. The mention of image is not to establish the value of man's life, but to establish man's right and duty to judge wrongdoing. The apostle Paul reflects on this in Romans 13 when he states that governing authorities bear the sword, even calling the governor "the servant of God, an avenger who carries out God's wrath on the wrongdoer" (v. 4).

The regulation of Genesis 9:6 is the covenantal foundation for God's instituting the state, that is, governments that regulate human society, particularly by protecting their lives. The state, imperfect as it is, is God's instituted means whereby he punishes wrongdoers, thereby restraining human depravity. This is why Peter and Paul can say what they do about the Roman government (Rom. 13; 1 Pet. 2).

This regulation further exhibits that God has preserved in humans a sense of law. Even though the inclination of man is evil from youth, God reveals his natural law on the conscience of men. Thus, Paul can say, "For when Gentiles, who do not have the law, by nature do what the law requires, they are a law to themselves, even though they do not have the law. They show that the work of the law is written on their hearts, while their conscience also bears witness" (Rom. 2:14–15). The Noahic covenant is the covenantal foundation for God ordering the world by natural law and preserving in fallen man an awareness of this law, so that man does not act as badly as he might.

These three regulations demonstrate that God ordered all of human life in the Noahic covenant. Fruitfulness covers the realm of marriage and family; food encapsulates the realm of vocation and enjoyment of good things; murder includes the arena of state and society; and natural law is evident in them all. Both Christians and non-Christians participate in all of these arenas, and all of these arenas are necessary to the preserving of human society. They are founded on the Noahic covenant and are an important part of the Christian life.

Continuity with Creation. The common grace covenant upholds and governs all of human history and the world. Nevertheless, to identify accurately the Noahic covenant as the covenantal foundation for all these regulations, we have to recognize the Noahic covenant's continuity with creation. We have already mentioned some of these connections, but it is worth giving a broader list here. The command to be fruitful and multiply repeats Genesis 1:28. The image of God mentioned in 9:6 ties with Genesis 1:26. The regulation that protects the life of man is similar to God's sign to Cain that protected his life from murder (Gen. 4:15). Jeremiah's mention of a covenant with day and night that recalls 8:22 is also reminiscent of God's call for the sun to rule the day (1:16–18). Humankind having to work for food links with God's curse in Genesis 3:17–19. Moreover, God's statement in 8:21, "I will not continue to curse the ground any further" (my translation), demonstrates that God is not changing his previous curse in 3:17.

Other connections could be listed, but the above illustrate that God is reinstating the natural order previous to the flood. There is an essential continuity in the created order before and after the flood. This is not to minimize the differences that Peter mentions in 2 Peter 3:5–7. Nonetheless, humanity is still in the image of God and imprisoned to the curse of sin and death. Seasons come and go as before. The theology of Genesis 1–4 still informs and guides our faith and life.

For the Seed to Come. Finally, the common grace covenant provides the arena for Christ to come. God promised Adam and Eve salvation through the coming Champion-Offspring. Had God destroyed the world completely, this promise would not have been fulfilled. The Lord's promise entails an ongoing conflict between the offspring of the Serpent and that of the woman, which needs a stage on which to unfold. It is the common grace realm secured in God's promise that provides this stage for the drama of redemptive history.

God's common grace sustains and upholds the natural order and human society so that Christ could be born of a woman, and under the law, in the fullness of time. After Christ's ascension, the Lord did not bring the final judgment. Instead, according to his great mercy, the Father ordained the second coming of Christ to be in the distant future, so that many more generations may be born, hear the gospel proclaimed to them, and receive the free salvation found in Christ. One day, without warning, the heavens will be torn in two like a newspaper. The sun will turn black as coal and the moon blood-red. The mountains, tall and solid, seemingly indestructible, will be picked up like rag dolls and thrown away. The islands that are locked down to the sea floor will be sent skipping across the sea like a smooth stone. With the same ease with which God spoke the world into existence, he will send in his demolition team to tear it down. Common grace will come to an end when that seventh trumpet is blown and Christ rides forth on his glorious chariot cloud.

But until that day, common grace serves the purpose of God's saving grace. As long as the sun shines, the gospel will be proclaimed, and those who were once lost will be found in Christ. Christ will continue to build his church, protecting her from the onslaughts of the Evil One, until he brings this world to a close.

Why Is This Doctrine Important for the Christian Life?

In the coming years, it is unlikely that Hollywood will stop unrolling its end-of-the-world films. Likewise, storms will keep crashing on the shores of our lives. The earthquakes, hurricanes, and volcanic eruptions will come with the seasons. The wickedness of humanity will continue to inflict evil and tragedy on society and this creation. Nevertheless, these dark storms clouds will once more part to display a blue sky painted with the colors of the rainbow. God will see his rainbow and keep his promise.

Therefore, the rainbow gives us assurance in the unshakeable promise of God. Whatever disasters lie in the future, there will be no more Noah figures, no more near world destructions. Rather, the rainbow reminds us that God will preserve winter and spring, marriage and childbirth, and human society until Christ comes in glory. The Noahic covenant comforts us with the assurance that nothing can thwart God's plan, and nothing can separate us from the love of God in Christ Jesus.

Questions for Further Reflection

1. Who are the parties of the Noahic covenant?
2. Explain how the Noahic covenant is non-redemptive.
3. What does the sign of the Noahic covenant symbolize?
4. List at least two of the regulations for humanity contained within the Noahic covenant.
5. Is it possible for humanity to break this covenant by its wickedness?
6. How does the Noahic covenant serve God's redemptive purpose?

5

I Will Give to You:
THE ABRAHAMIC COVENANT

In the opening scenes to Peter Jackson's film adaptation of Tolkien's *Fellowship of the Ring*, a narrator sets up the plot of the story by giving the viewer a condensed history lesson on the mythological world of Middle Earth. The movie touches on critical events over thousands of years of history, explaining the significance of Sauron's ring and how it fell into the hands of a hobbit named Bilbo. Once the prologue is complete and the plot is made clear, the speed of the camera slows down, and the story focuses on its central character, Frodo, the nephew of Bilbo, who must destroy the ring.

The book of Genesis unfolds in a similar way. Although it is true history and not mythology, the first eleven chapters are an overview of ancient history, a prologue leading up to the central character of the story: Abraham. Once Abraham is introduced, the speed of the camera slows down, as it were, and the narrator focuses on the covenant that God made with him and his offspring, a covenant that is predominant to the plot of redemptive history and the unity of the Scriptures.

What Is the Abrahamic Covenant?

Although the covenant of grace began with God's promise in Genesis 3:15, it is more fully revealed in the Abrahamic covenant. As Meredith Kline said, "Redemptive history enters a distinctive new stage with the Abrahamic Covenant but without interrupting the underlying continuity and coherence of the Covenant of Grace

... God's covenantal transactions with Abraham stand in solid continuity with the pre-Abrahamic past and the messianic future."[1] In other words, the Abrahamic covenant is the particular and historical establishment of the one underlying covenant of grace, for it is out of this covenant that the old and new covenants come.

In chapter 3, we pointed out briefly that God promised Abraham an offspring and a land, and he fulfilled these promises in two stages. The first stage of fulfillment is in the old covenant, with the nation Israel and the land of Canaan. Israel was the promised offspring, and Canaan was the Promised Land. These promises, however, were not an end in themselves, for God also promised Abraham that through him he would bless the nations. The second, and greater, stage of fulfillment is in the new covenant. God's promise of an offspring is fulfilled in believers and their children, and his promise of a land looks forward to the greater fulfillment of the new heavens and new earth. The nation of Israel and the land of Canaan were only temporary, first-level fulfillments of God's promises to Abraham. With the coming of Christ, a greater fulfillment has occurred.

A visual sketch of this two-stage fulfillment is shown in Figure 3.

Figure 3. Fulfillment of Abrahamic Covenant in Two Stages

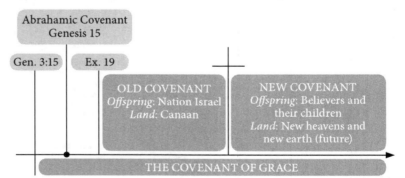

As this diagram shows, the Abrahamic covenant was not interrupted by God's national covenant with Israel at Sinai (typically called the Mosaic or *old* covenant), but runs continuously until its fulfillment in the new covenant. In fact, it has such tight continuity

---

1. Kline, *Kingdom Prologue*, 292.

with the new covenant that the New Testament writers deliberately call Christians—whether Jew or Gentile—the offspring of Abraham. In Galatians 3:29, for example, Paul says, "And if you are Christ's, then you are Abraham's offspring, heirs according to promise" (see also Rom. 4:11; Heb. 2:16). Christians today from every tongue, nation, and tribe in the world are the heirs of God's promises to Abraham. Those promises were fulfilled in Christ, who is Abraham's Offspring (Gal. 3:16) and the One who inaugurated the new covenant. God made us heirs, not because of our obedience to the law, but because of Christ's obedience, which is imputed to us freely of his grace. He is the one Mediator of the one covenant of grace as it is administered in both the Abrahamic and new covenants. As Calvin observed, "This covenant [that is, the Abrahamic] is so much like ours [that is, the new] in substance and reality, that the two are actually one and the same."[2] Both are covenants of promise, not law. In both, God promises to give gifts to undeserving sinners on the basis of his grace through Christ alone. Thus, Calvin was correct to say that "the covenant made with Abraham is no less in force today for Christians than it was of old for Jewish people."[3] The substance of the covenant has not changed.

As we will see in the next chapter, the Mosaic covenant, which came after the Abrahamic covenant, played an important role in the fulfillment of God's promises to Abraham, yet it was different in administration. While it was still an administration of the one covenant of grace, the Mosaic covenant had a principle of law. Whereas the Abrahamic covenant promised, "I will give to you" (Gen. 15; 17:7–8; 22:16–18; 26:3–4, 24; 28:13–15), the Mosaic covenant threatened, "Cursed be everyone who does not abide by all things written in the Book of the Law, and do them" (Gal. 3:10b; Lev. 18:5; cf. Deut. 27:26). Whereas faith in the promise given in Abraham justified sinners (Gal. 3:6–9), obedience to the law did not (Gal. 3:11–12). Those who were justified during the time of the Mosaic covenant were so because their faith was in the promise of the Abrahamic covenant. The Mosaic covenant in no way superseded or abrogated the Abrahamic covenant, for "the law," says Paul, "which came 430

---

2. *Institutes*, 2.10.2.
3. *Institutes*, 4.16.6.

years afterward, does not annul a covenant previously ratified by God, so as to make the promise void. For if the inheritance comes by the law, it no longer comes by promise; but God gave it to Abraham by promise" (Gal. 3:17–18).

This naturally leads one to ask, "Well, why then did God give the Mosaic covenant in the first place?" This, of course, is precisely the rhetorical question that Paul asks in Galatians 3:19: "Why then the law?" Paul says it was *added* to the covenant already in place (that is, the Abrahamic covenant) because of sin, until the coming of Christ. The Mosaic covenant was like a tutor to children until those children had grown (see Gal. 3:23–26). To put it another way, it was like training wheels on a bicycle. Training wheels serve the temporary purpose of helping a child learn how to ride a bike. Once a child has enough balance to keep the bike from tipping over, the training wheels come off. As long as those training wheels remain on the bike, its intended purpose cannot be fulfilled. The fulfillment of their intended purpose only comes when they are removed and the child moves on to better things. Similarly, the Mosaic covenant was only necessary for a time. As long as it remained in place, God's promise to Abraham was limited to the people of Israel and the land of Canaan. The greater fulfillment of these promises could not come until Christ fulfilled the Mosaic covenant and inaugurated the new.

Because Reformed theology has understood that the Abrahamic and new covenants are both covenants of promise and that they share a tight continuity with one another, it has also understood the children of believers to be members of the covenant of grace and rightful recipients of the covenant sign of baptism. The Heidelberg Catechism, for example, after its five questions dealing with the sacrament of baptism in general, asks in Question 74:

> Q: Are infants also to be baptized?
>
> A: Yes. For since they, as well as their parents, belong to the covenant and people of God, and both redemption from sin and the Holy Spirit, who works faith, are through the blood of Christ promised to them no less than to their parents; they are also by baptism, as a sign of the covenant, to be ingrafted into the Christian Church, and distinguished from the children of

unbelievers, as was done in the Old Covenant by circumcision, in place of which in the New Covenant baptism is appointed.

Just as God appointed a covenant sign of inclusion in the Abrahamic covenant (circumcision), he also appointed a covenant sign of inclusion in the new covenant (baptism). If God included the children of believers into the Abrahamic covenant, there is no reason to assume that he has not done the same in the new covenant. The Reformed theologian B. B. Warfield (1851–1921) stated this point quite plainly:

> The argument [of infant baptism] in a nutshell is simply this: God established his church in the days of Abraham and put children into it. They must remain there until he puts them out. He has nowhere put them out. They are still then members of his church and as such entitled to its ordinances.[4]

Clearly, the New Testament has no such command to remove the children of believers from his covenant. On the contrary, we find Jesus saying, "Let the little children come to me and do not hinder them, for to such belongs the kingdom of heaven" (Matt. 19:14).

How should we then define the Abrahamic covenant? We define it as *the covenant of grace established with Abraham and his offspring, wherein God promised the entire future of his covenantal kingdom, in both its old covenant and new covenant stages.*[5]

What Does the Bible Teach?

The Abrahamic covenant begins in Genesis 12 with God's sovereign call of Abraham (then named Abram):

> Go from your country and your kindred and your father's house to the land that I will show you. And I will make of you a great nation, and I will bless you and make your name great, so that you will be a blessing. I will bless those who bless you, and him who dishonors you I will curse, and in you all the families of the earth shall be blessed. (Gen. 12:1–3)

---

4. B. B. Warfield, "The Polemics of Infant Baptism," in *Studies in Theology* (1932; reprint, Grand Rapids: Baker, 1981), 9.408

5. see Kline, *Kingdom Prologue*, 293.

It is important to notice that this was not a joint or bilateral agreement between God and Abraham. They did not sit down at the bargaining table to negotiate a covenant between them. Rather, this was a unilateral act performed by God, in which he chose Abraham (and not one of Abraham's neighbors in Ur) and made unconditional promises to him: "I will . . . I will . . . I will." From beginning to end, it was all of God's sovereign grace.

That these unconditional promises are God's covenant with Abraham becomes clearer in Genesis 15 with the ratification ceremony of this covenant. God's promise to give Abraham an offspring begins in verse 1, where he says in a vision, "Fear not, Abram, I am your shield: your reward will be very great." This reward is God's unilateral grant to Abraham, which he had already promised in chapter 12.

But Abraham is concerned about this promise. He has no children of his own, and he is old and well past the age of fathering a child. This troubles Abraham, because he has no offspring to inherit any reward the Lord gave him. What use would it be, given his old age and childless status? So Abraham respectfully objects: "O Lord God . . . the heir of my house is Eliezer of Damascus . . . you have given me no offspring." In other words, because he had no son, Abraham would have to adopt a servant in his house to be his heir, which in his culture was a common practice for a childless man. The Lord responds to Abraham's objection in verse 4 by saying, "This man shall not be your heir; your very own son shall be your heir." He then reassures Abraham by bringing him outside and saying, "Look toward heaven, and number the stars, if you are able to number them . . . so shall your offspring be." Of course, he is not able to number them, for who can number the stars? God made his point: childless Abraham would have more offspring than he could possibly number.

This promise must seem impossible to Abraham. He is nearly one hundred years old at this point. Although he wanted children, he has probably resigned himself to the fact that he will not have any, since he and his wife Sarah are old enough to be great-grandparents. Considering this, we could sympathize with Abraham if he had responded to the Lord's promise with a "Yeah, right! I'll believe it when I see it." Yet verse 6 tells us that he responds in exactly the opposite manner. Abraham "believed the LORD, and he counted it to him as righteousness." It seemed impossible, and maybe even a little crazy, but it was the promise of the Lord nonetheless. Abraham trusted the Lord and, through faith alone, was justified (see also Rom. 4).

The Lord, however, is not finished yet. Not only does he promise offspring to Abraham but he also promises him a land to possess. Again, we are told that Abraham wants some sort of assurance that this will be so. He says in verse 8, "O Lord God, how am I to know that I shall possess it?" God then accommodates Abraham further by sealing this promise with a solemn covenant ritual. "You want a guarantee, Abraham? Go get a three-year old heifer, a three-year old female goat, a three-year old ram, a turtledove, and a young pigeon."

This ritual was not a sacrifice. Rather, this was a blood-oath for a covenant ceremony. In Abraham's day, this was standard procedure for covenant-making. When two kings, or any other parties for that matter, made a treaty and covenant with each other, it was common practice to make some sort of blood-oath after explaining the conditions of the covenant, including the promised reward for keeping the covenant and the penalties for breaking it. As part of the covenant ceremony, animals would be killed and sometimes cut into two. Typically, the lesser of the two kings (often referred to as a "vassal"), the one considered the servant of the other king (often referred to as a "suzerain"), would take an oath and walk between the animals or do some other type of ritual in which he would promise to keep the covenant. Such an oath was gravely serious, for to pass through the rows of severed carcasses was essentially to walk through the valley of the shadow of death. The person taking the oath was saying that if he broke the covenant, he would become just like that severed animal.

Abraham understood this ritual. In his day, this was how people made and ratified covenants. What is so amazing about this particular covenant, however, is that God, the Lord of the covenant, assumed the full obligations to fulfill his promise symbolized in this covenant ritual by walking *alone* through the severed animals. He manifests his presence in a smoking fire pot and flaming torch and passes between the carcasses. A cloud of smoke that arises from the fire pot and a soaring flame that comes from the torch are symbolic forms of the Lord's presence, similar to those forms he used during the exodus: a pillar of cloud and a pillar of fire. By walking alone between the severed animal halves, the Lord takes a blood-oath and invokes death upon himself, should he fail to fulfill his promise (see Jer. 34:18). Abraham does not walk through the carcasses; thus no obligations are imposed on him. The Lord makes this unilateral covenant of promise and seals it with an oath.

First stage of fulfillment. As redemptive history unfolds in the pages of the Old and New Testaments, the Bible reveals that the fulfillment of God's promises to Abraham come in two marvelous stages. As we mentioned above, the first stage of fulfillment comes in the history of the nation Israel. Genesis 21 tells us that the Lord finally gives Abraham and Sarah a son, Isaac. Although it seems impossible that such a thing should happen, God fulfills his promise. From Isaac comes Jacob (later named Israel), and from Jacob come his twelve sons, who father the twelve tribes of Israel. God renews the Abrahamic covenant with Isaac (Gen. 26:1–5) and Jacob (Gen. 28:10–17).

As the story progresses, we learn how these descendants of Abraham all end up in Egypt, where they continue to multiply generation after generation. In fact, the book of Exodus begins by describing how the people of Israel "increased greatly . . . and grew exceedingly strong, so that the land of Egypt was filled with them" (Ex. 1:7b). They become so numerous that Pharaoh becomes afraid and begins to afflict them with heavy burdens and puts them in slavery for four hundred years, just as God foretold in Genesis 15:13. Moses reminds Israel that their large population is the fulfillment of God's promise to father Abraham: "The LORD your God has multiplied you, and behold, you are today as numerous as the stars of heaven" (Deut. 1:10). He fulfills his promise to give Abraham an offspring numbered like the stars. The Bible reaffirms this fulfillment again during the reign of Solomon, when "Judah and Israel were as many as the sand by the sea" (1 Kings 4:20a; cf. 1 Kings 3:8; Gen. 22:17; 32:12).

As the story continues to develop, the Bible reveals God's fulfillment of his promise regarding the land. Under the leadership of Joshua, Israel enters the promised land of Canaan and takes possession of it by driving out the heathen. Joshua 21:43–45 tells us that this is the fulfillment of God's promise.

Thus the LORD gave to Israel all the land that he swore to give to their fathers. And they took possession of it, and they settled there. And the LORD gave them rest on every side just as he had sworn to their fathers. Not one of all their enemies had withstood them, for the LORD had given all their enemies into their hands. Not one word of all the good promises that the LORD had made to the house of Israel had failed; all came to pass.

Just as God fulfilled his promise to give Abraham an offspring, he also fulfills his promise to give his offspring the land.

Second stage of fulfillment. As marvelous as these fulfilled promises were, however, they were only the first level of fulfillment. The nation Israel and the land of Canaan were only pictures and foreshadows of a far greater fulfillment revealed in the New Testament. This fulfillment was the result of Christ's person and work.

In the fullness of time, Christ, whom Paul calls the Offspring of Abraham (Gal. 3:16), came into the world to fulfill the work the Father gave him to do, which included suffering the curse pictured in the covenantal blood-oath of Genesis 15. Not only did Christ live a life of perfect obedience in our place but he also had to become like those bloodied, severed animals; that is, he had to become a curse for our sin (Gal. 3:13). There was no other way to redeem his people and give us access to righteousness, eternal life, and the glory of the age to come. On the cross, his flesh was torn and his blood was shed as he suffered the judgment of God's holy wrath against our sin. In other words, God's blood-oath in Genesis 15 was his commitment to the death of Christ for our sins. The promises made to Abraham could be fulfilled in no other way.

Upon the completion of Christ's work, God's promises to Abraham enter their second stage of fulfillment. Galatians 3, for example, reveals the second stage of fulfillment concerning God's promise to give Abraham offspring. In making his argument against the Judaizers that salvation is through faith alone in Christ alone, and not by works of the law, Paul is careful to show how one becomes a true descendant of Abraham. In Galatians 3:7–9 he says,

> Know then that it is those of faith who are the sons of Abraham. And the Scripture, foreseeing that God would justify the Gentiles by faith, preached the gospel beforehand to Abraham, saying, "In

you shall all the nations of the earth be blessed." So then, those who are of faith are blessed along with Abraham, the man of faith.

Justification happens in the same way now to people of every tongue, nation, and tribe as it did to Abraham: by faith alone.

The promise goes out to all the earth because of what Paul says in verse 16: "Now the promises were made to Abraham and to his offspring. It does not say, 'And to offsprings,' referring to many, but referring to one, 'And to your offspring,' who is Christ." Paul uses a play on words to draw an important conclusion: Christ is the offspring of Abraham, through whom all the promises come to us who believe. Even the law that was given through Moses 430 years later could not annul the covenant previously made to Abraham and ratified in blood (see Gal. 3:17). That promise is fulfilled in Christ: "If you are Christ's, then you are Abraham's offspring, heirs according to the promise" (3:29). The message of the New Testament is clear: the great number of offspring promised to Abraham was only foreshadowed in national Israel. Therefore, not all of national Israel is of true Israel. Those who are truly offspring of Abraham are those who, like Abraham, are justified through faith alone in the Offspring (Christ) alone.

But what about the promise of a land? How is that fulfilled on a greater level? Again, the New Testament reveals to us a reality that is fuller than the type and shadow of the Old Covenant. Notice what Hebrews 11 tells us:

> By faith Abraham obeyed when he was called to go out to a place that he was to receive as an inheritance. And he went out, not knowing where he was going. By faith he went to live in the land of promise, as in a foreign land, living in tents with Isaac and Jacob, heirs with him of the same promise. For he was looking forward to the city that has foundations, whose builder and designer is God . . . These all died in faith, not having received the things promised, but having seen them and greeted them from afar, and having acknowledged that they were strangers and exiles on the earth. For people who speak thus make it clear that they are seeking a homeland. If they had been thinking of that land from which they had gone out, they would have had opportunity to return. But as it is, they desire a better country,

that is, a heavenly one. Therefore God is not ashamed to be called their God, for he has prepared for them a city (vv. 8–10, 13–16).

The promised land of Canaan was temporary, not permanent. The permanent Promised Land is the heavenly country that still awaits us, a land that is infinitely greater than any plot of real estate in this present age. What awaits us is the new heaven and new earth. While the nation Israel received a good land, ultimately it became corrupt, defiled, and it faded away. The greater Promised Land, however, is an inheritance that Peter says is "incorruptible, undefiled, unfading, kept in heaven for you" (1 Pet. 1:4). And like our father Abraham, we look forward to this inheritance with hope.

The continuity of the covenant. What does all of this promise and fulfillment show us? It shows us that there is continuity in the *one* plan of salvation for the *one* people of God, whom the Bible describes as the seed or offspring of Abraham (Gal. 3:29). There is no other way to be a child of God than to be included into Abraham's covenant. Thus, when Reformed people speak of "*the* covenant," we are speaking of the one covenant of grace that runs from its seed-promise in Genesis 3:15, was expanded in detail to Abraham in Genesis 15, fulfilled in Christ, and continues throughout time until the consummation. Anyone who has or ever will be saved—in any period of human history—is a member of this one covenant of grace. Salvation is always the same: by grace alone, through faith alone, because of the one Mediator of the covenant alone, the Lord Jesus Christ.

The inclusion of children. This continuity in the one covenant of grace also shows us that God includes the children of believers in his covenant. In Genesis 17, God reminded Abraham of the promises he made in his covenant, which extended to his offspring (see 17:6–8). He then commanded that a sign of his covenant be given to Abraham and his descendants. Genesis 17:9–14 tells us:

> And God said to Abraham, "As for you, you shall keep my covenant, you and your offspring after you throughout their generations. This is my covenant, which you shall keep, between me and you and your offspring after you: Every male among you shall be circumcised. You shall be circumcised in the flesh of your foreskins, and it shall be a sign of the covenant between me and you. He who is eight days old

among you shall be circumcised. Every male throughout your generations, whether born in your house or bought with your money from any foreigner who is not of your offspring, both he who is born in your house or bought with your money, shall surely be circumcised. So shall my covenant be in your flesh an everlasting covenant. Any uncircumcised male who is not circumcised in the flesh of his foreskin shall be cut off from his people; he has broken my covenant."

Circumcision was a "sign of the covenant" that showed God's people that he chose them as his own. The bloody ritual of cutting the flesh in the male reproductive organ signified God's covenant with Abraham when he walked between the bloody animal halves. Every male in Abraham's household, whether sons or servants, as well as every male in the covenant community thereafter, was to have this sign carved in his flesh as a constant reminder of God's promises to Abraham and his descendants. This was no mere formality; rather, to be circumcised meant to receive a sign of the deepest spiritual significance (Rom. 4:11). It also consecrated the individual to the Lord as a member of his covenant people. Conversely, anyone who rejected the sign of the covenant was to be cut off from the covenant community. To reject the *sign* of the covenant was to reject God's *promises* in the covenant. Ultimately, it was an act of unbelief. To reject circumcision was to refuse fellowship with the God who walked between the severed animal halves and made an oath to his people.

With the coming of Christ, however, circumcision is no longer the appropriate sign of God's covenant of grace, for Christ fulfilled it when he was "cut off from the land of the living" in his crucifixion (Isa. 53:8). Because he was our bloody circumcision on the cross, the covenant sign of inclusion changed from circumcision to baptism. Paul makes this equation in Colossians 2:11–12:

> In him also you were circumcised with a circumcision made without hands, by putting off the body of the flesh, by the circumcision of Christ, having been buried with him in baptism, in which you were also raised with him through faith in the powerful working of God, who raised him from the dead.

Circumcision is no longer the sign of the covenant because Christ *was* our circumcision. Thus, in the new covenant, the covenantal sign administered upon initiation into the visible church is no longer circumcision but baptism, a sign that identifies us with Christ's death, burial, and resurrection. Like circumcision, baptism is a one-time, initiatory sign and seal of God's covenant promise, marking out an individual as belonging to God's covenant people.

Yet, unlike circumcision, baptism is applied to females as well as males (Acts 8:12). In the new covenant, there is greater inclusion into the covenant people of God than in the old covenant. Gentiles who were not of the physical family of Abraham and were "separated from Christ, alienated from the commonwealth of Israel and strangers to the covenants of promise, having no hope and without God in the world" (Eph. 2:12) are in the new covenant "no longer strangers and aliens, but . . . are fellow citizens with the saints and members of the household of God" (Eph. 2:19). Likewise, females as well as males receive the covenant sign of inclusion into the new covenant. As Paul says, "there is neither Jew nor Greek . . . there is neither male nor female, for you are all one in Christ Jesus" (Gal. 3:28).

Like circumcision, however, baptism is for the believer *and his children*. In the new covenant, God still claims for himself a covenant people, not only adult converts. The pattern he established in the Abrahamic covenant continues into the new. This is why Peter said in his announcement at the Feast of Pentecost, "Repent and be baptized every one of you in the name of Jesus Christ for the forgiveness of sins, and you will receive the gift of the Holy Spirit. For the promise is for you *and for your children* and for all who are far off, everyone whom the Lord our God calls to himself" (Acts 2:38–39; emphasis added). Those who are "far off" are the Gentiles, now included into God's covenant. But notice that Peter specifically points out that the promise is also "for your children." Children of believers are not excluded from membership in God's covenant community but included, just as they were since the beginning.

For this reason, Paul addresses the children of believers as members of the covenant of grace: "Children, obey your parents in the Lord" (Eph. 6:1). He even reminds them of the fifth commandment in the very next verse, showing that new covenant children have the same

> Our responsibility is to baptise children into the visible church of God's covenant people — Only God knows who's in the invisible church

privileges as old covenant children, only greater.[6] They are to be raised as disciples of Christ: "Fathers, do not provoke your children to anger, but bring them up in the discipline and instruction of the Lord" (Eph. 6:4; cf. Deut. 6:4–9). Clearly, these children are considered members of the visible church, no less than they were in the old covenant. As such, they should receive the sign of the covenant and be baptized.

Why Is This Doctrine Important for the Christian Life?

1. The doctrine of the Abrahamic covenant is important for several reasons. First, it shows us that God is a God of promise. It reveals to us what he is like in his nature by showing us how he has acted toward his people in history. This is vital for our faith as we travel through this wilderness age like pilgrims, looking to the promised land of the new heavens and new earth. Often, we are like Israel in the desert, tempted to disbelieve the Lord's promises and doubt his goodness. We are tempted to grumble and complain against the Lord for not satisfying our shopping list of felt needs. The doctrine of the Abrahamic covenant, however, calls us out of our self-centeredness and disbelief by displaying before our eyes the God who keeps his promises and has taken us to be his covenant people. It directs our faith to Christ, in whom all of God's promises are "yes" and "amen," and tells us that, even though we live in a world filled with letdowns and broken promises, God will never go back on his word. Even though we will experience hardship and suffering in this life, his promises do not change. He will remember our sins no more. He will cause us to persevere in the faith, finish in us the good work he began, and resurrect our bodies from the dead. He will bring us to that heavenly country to which all of God's saints and spiritual descendants of Abraham have looked, that country wherein only righteousness dwells, where there is no crying or sadness or pain, and nothing evil or corrupt will ever enter its gates. We can look with great hope to the future and rest in the promises of God, for they always come to pass.

2. Second, the doctrine of the Abrahamic covenant assures our faith by highlighting the work of Christ, the Offspring of Abraham.

---

6. We should keep in mind that Paul's epistles were read to the whole congregation when they assembled together for worship (see 1 Thess. 5:27; Col. 4:16).

Because Christ was made a curse for us and suffered the realities of the blood-oath of Genesis 15, we have confidence that we are no longer under a curse and have been redeemed from the curse of the law (Gal. 3:13). Knowing this is essential to our joy as Christians as well as living a life of grateful obedience. If we think we are still under God's curse because of our sin, we will inevitably be driven to serve God out of servile fear rather than grateful and joyful obedience. We will constantly relate to God by the law and attempt to earn his favor. But the doctrine of the Abrahamic covenant shows us that, in Christ, we have been made Abraham's offspring and heirs according to God's promise (Gal. 3:29). It announces good news to us by telling us that we have been given eternal life and access into the holy presence of God. As Hebrews 10:19–20 says, we now "have confidence to enter the holy places by the blood of Jesus, by the new and living way that he opened for us through the curtain, that is, through his flesh."

Third, the doctrine of the Abrahamic covenant declares God's grace to the nations. It tells us that the gospel is for people of every race, tribe, and nationality. God promised Abraham that he would be a light to the nations, and indeed that has come to pass. It is because of God's promise to Abraham that the apostles were sent as Christ's witnesses not only in Jerusalem and in all Judea but also in Samaria and to the end of the earth (Acts 1:8). It is because of God's promise to Abraham that Christians are black, white, Asian, Hispanic, and more. The Christian faith is not a northern European faith, nor a Semitic faith, but an international, global faith in which "there is neither Jew nor Greek, there is neither slave nor free, there is neither male nor female, for you are all one in Christ Jesus" (Gal. 3:28). In a world that is typically segregated by our cultural identities, consumer preferences, and political affiliations, the doctrine of the Abrahamic covenant shows us that the church, as it is gathered throughout the world, is "a chosen race, a royal priesthood, a holy nation, a people for his own possession" (1 Pet. 2:9a). Nothing but the gospel can create a community like this one.

Fourth, the doctrine of the Abrahamic covenant tells us that God claims the children of believers as part of his covenant community and should be regarded as heirs of his promises. Baptism, of course, does not save them (or anyone), for faith, not baptism, is the instrument whereby the righteousness of Christ is received and imputed to a sinner. Yet baptism is God's sacrament of inclusion into his covenant of grace, and by it God promises salvation to those who believe. The doctrine of the Abrahamic covenant helps Christian parents view their children as rightful recipients of this covenant sign and thus God's heirs of his covenant. It helps parents understand more clearly their role as stewards of these children who must be brought up in the training and admonition of the Lord.

Questions for Further Reflection

1. Why did the Lord walk between the severed animal pieces in Genesis 15? *to seal the cov. c̄ Abraham*

2. How was God's promise to give Abraham an offspring fulfilled in the old covenant? *Israel in Canaan*

3. How was God's promise to give Abraham an offspring fulfilled on a greater level in the new covenant? *Christians – in Christ*

4. How was God's promise to give Abraham's offspring a land fulfilled in the old covenant? *Canaan*

5. How was God's promise to give Abraham's offspring a land fulfilled on a greater level in the new covenant? *New Heavens & earth*

6. How does the covenant sign of circumcision correspond to the covenant sign of baptism? *inclusion in visible church*

7. How does it comfort you to know that, as a Christian, you are a child of Abraham? *I cannot lose the inheritance of a child of God.*

6

Don't Spare the Rod:
LAW SERVING GRACE IN THE MOSAIC COVENANT

If you open your Bible at random, it's quite likely that you will land in the Old Testament. Like Jupiter to the earth, the Old Testament dwarfs the New Testament by the sheer number of its words. Yet the vastness of the Old Testament orb rarely influences our piety proportionally. How often do you read the Old Testament in your devotions? Pastors spend most of their ministries preaching in the New Testament, and many churches almost avoid the Old Testament altogether. Sermons on the Old Testament are like an exhibit of spiders at the zoo: intriguing but a bit scary. And when we do venture into the Old Testament, we treat it like eating at a cafeteria, picking the few things that look safe and leaving the rest. The church's piety has come to resemble a Gideon's Pocket Bible, containing only the New Testament, the Psalms, and Proverbs. With the exception of certain stories like David and Goliath or Daniel and the lions' den, the majority of the Old Testament has died the death of old family photos: they are kept around, but no one recognizes the people in the pictures anymore.

Of course, there are plenty of good reasons for our preoccupation with the New Testament. If the Bible were a building, the New Testament would be the penthouse suite; it reveals in glory and clarity Jesus Christ, our only Lord and Savior. The gospel in all its simple sweetness graces the pages of the Greek portion of Holy Scripture. Without it, the Old Testament would remain largely veiled to us, and we would see Christ only dimly. And yet, if the New Testament is the second-story penthouse suite, then the Old Testament is the foundation and ground floor. What chance does the second story have of surviving if the first story is not kept up? Without the ground floor, the second level crashes down. The Old Testament is the rock on which the New Testament rests. Without it, the New Testament is left upon the sand.

Our misunderstanding of much of the New Testament is a direct result of our lack of proper instruction in the Old Testament. Widespread ignorance of the Old Testament has left the church and our Christian piety in an anemic state. And the most misunderstood part of the Old Testament is the covenant God made with Israel at Sinai, hereafter called the Mosaic covenant. The dominance of this covenant in the Old Testament can hardly be overemphasized. The very name *Old Testament* means the old covenant of Sinai compared to the new covenant. Thus, virtually every Old Testament book, in one way or another, falls under the Mosaic covenant. (Genesis is not properly under the Sinai covenant, but it is a prologue to it.) Thus, our comprehension of the Old Testament depends on our proficiency in the Mosaic covenant. This covenant is the arterial system of the Old Testament and is essential to the well-being of our faith.

So then, what is the Mosaic covenant about? Why the Mosaic covenant? What were God's purposes and plans in the Mosaic covenant? How does it form the foundation that is so crucial to the gospel of Jesus Christ? All of these questions and more are answered by an examination of the Mosaic covenant, which will make the whole Bible, both its Old and New Testaments, come alive for the benefit of your faith. <u>The Mosaic covenant will make you cling ever tighter in love to your Savior Jesus Christ</u>.

What Is the Mosaic Covenant?

To understand the Mosaic covenant properly, we must view it in both its broad and narrow senses. <u>In its broad sense, the Mosaic covenant is an administration of the covenant of grace. God's ultimate purpose for the Mosaic covenant was to lead his people to Christ for salvation</u>. The Israelites were saved by the grace of God in Jesus Christ as they looked to him through faith. The Israelites in no way earned their eternal salvation but received it as a gift through Christ.

In its narrow sense, however, the Mosaic covenant is a covenant of law. The means by which God led Israel to Christ was through his demands of obedience to the terms of the covenant upon which physical blessings or curses were received. This narrow sense of the Mosaic covenant must not be dismissed or watered down in light of its broad sense. We must first focus on the Mosaic covenant in its narrower sense (that is, law) to fit it properly into God's overall purpose of the covenant of grace.

This leads us to ask, why did God administer the covenant of grace by law under the Mosaic covenant? The answer to this question touches on the center of how it is possible for God to redeem sinful man. Salvation is ultimately about us living with our holy God in heaven; it is communion with God in glory. How, though, is this possible? The only way sinful humans can live in the presence of the holy God is for them to be made holy like God. As Hebrews 12:14 tells us, without holiness no one will see God. God is holy and just, and his love and grace in no way change this. The only way we will ever get to heaven and enjoy everlasting peace and life with God is for us to be perfectly righteous and holy. There is no other way.

This is what Jesus proves by his conversation with the rich young ruler (Matt. 19:16–23; Luke 18:18–24). Jesus demonstrates that the only way to have everlasting life is to obey God's law perfectly. To this the disciples respond, "Who then can be saved?" Jesus answers, "With man this is impossible, but with God all things are possible." Our problem is that we fail to appreciate this truth fully. Our tendency is to think we can obey, that we can become holy by our own efforts. We do this in two primary ways. First, we attempt to dilute God's righteousness by lowering his standard of holiness and assuming that God values our works. Or second, we are prone to assume that we are not that sinful, that if we really try and if we get a little help our obedience will make us holy. The destination, however, is the same for both avenues, the destruction of the biblical doctrine of salvation. Hence, God gave humanity the Mosaic covenant to help with this serious problem. In the written record of the lives of real people and the history of a nation, God reveals in the Mosaic covenant his inapproachable holiness and the impossibility for sinful humanity to be saved by works. In short, through the Mosaic covenant, God shows our utter need of Christ.

Perhaps an analogy will help us to understand this better. Once there was a teenage boy who received a classic Ford Mustang from his grandfather; Yet the Mustang required a full restoration. The engine needed to be rebuilt, the body required repair and paint, and the interior demanded a total makeover. When the boy received the gift, his father offered to help him with the project. However, the teenage son in his arrogance turned his father down. The son insisted, even boasted, that he could do the whole job by himself. Having some experience with cars, he naively thought he could do it. The father tried to persuade his son that he would need help, showing him the long list of specifications he would have to meet perfectly for the car to run and be road legal. But the boy would not listen. In his conquer-the-world attitude, the youth was confident he could do it. Thus, the father, to teach his son a lesson, told his son that he was not going to help at all: no advice, suggestions, or aid whatsoever. The father made the son do the whole job perfectly in order to get his license. The father knew the son would fail and that it would cause more work for him in the end. Nonetheless, this was the only way for the son to learn and be humbled. After months in the garage with countless do-overs, the son dragged himself to the father in tears, begging for help. The dad looked at the son's work. There were runs in the paint, the engine would not start, the rear brakes were put together improperly, and the seats were atrocious. The car was almost in worse condition than when he started.

This story is very similar to the Mosaic covenant. The father made the son fix the car by himself out of love, because the son arrogantly thought he could do it. The father's strictness served his love for his son. The son did not accept his limits, and he did not appreciate the high standards he had to meet. Likewise, God gave the strict Mosaic covenant to show Israel and all humanity that no man can be justified by the works of the law (Rom. 3:19–20). The Father's laying down the law and the son's inevitable failure were ultimately for the son's good. Paul's summary of the law is paradigmatic for us: "The law was our guardian until Christ came, in order that we might be justified by faith" (Gal. 3:24).

Historically, Reformed theology has understood the Mosaic covenant in this way. For example, Zacharias Ursinus (1534–83), the chief author of the Heidelberg Catechism, said that the Mosaic covenant "teaches what we ought to be in order that we may be saved" and "promises eternal life and all good things on the condition of our own and perfect righteousness, and of obedience in us." This is to be contrasted with the gospel, which reveals God's promised blessings "upon the condition that we exercise faith in Christ, by which we embrace the obedience which another, even Christ, has performed in our behalf."[1] In other words, the Mosaic covenant drives us to Christ.

Caspar Olevianus (1536–87), the Catechism's other author, called the Mosaic covenant a "legal covenant" that "repeated and renewed" the covenant of works.[2] He correlated the command in the covenant of works (that is, "Do this and live") to the command in the Mosaic law (Lev. 18:5). The law, whether published in creation or republished in Sinai, demands perfect obedience and drives the repentant sinner to Christ in preparation to hear the gospel and to receive it by faith.

Likewise, Reformed authors such as Robert Rollock (1555–99), William Perkins (1558–1602), Amandus Polanus (1561–1610), Johannes Wollebius (1586–1629), Richard Sibbes (1577–1635), Samuel Bolton (1606–54), William Strong (d.1654), James Ussher (1561–1656), Johannes Cocceius (1603–69), Patrick Gillespie (1617–75), John Owen (1616–83), Francis Turretin (1623–87), and Herman Witsius (1636–1708) all taught that the Mosaic covenant was pedagogical and subservient to the salvific purposes of the covenant of grace.[3]

---

1. Ursinus, *Commentary*, 497.
2. Olevianus, *A Firm Foundation*, 9.
3. Robert Rollock, *A Treatise of our Effectual Calling* in *Select Works of Robert Rollock*, vol. 1, ed. W. M. Gunn (Edinburgh: Wodrow Society, 1849), 33–46; William Perkins, *A Golden Chaine* (London, 1591), 26; idem, *The Workes of That famous and worthy Minister of Christ in the Universitie of Cambridge, Mr. William Perkins* (London, 1616–18), 1:154; Amandus Polanus, *The Substance of Christian Religion*, trans. E.W. (London, 1595), 88; Johannes Wollebius, *Compendium Theologiae Christianae* (1626) in John W. Beardslee [ed. and trans.] *Reformed Dogmatics: J. Wollebius, G. Voetius and F. Turretin* (New York: OUP, 1965), 119; Richard Sibbes, *The Bruised Reed and Smoking Flax* in *The Works of Richard Sibbes* (Edinburgh: Banner of Truth, 1973), 1:58–59; Samuel Bolton, *The True Bounds of Christian Freedome* (London, 1645), 145; William Strong, *A Discourse of the Two Covenants* (London, 1678), 88; James Ussher, *A Body of Divinity Or Summe and Substance of Religion*, 2nd Edition (London: 1653), 123–24, 158; Johannes Cocceius, *Summa Doctrinae De Foedere Et Testamento Dei* (Leiden, 1660), §13, 334–48; Patrick

How should we then define the Mosaic covenant? *The Mosaic covenant is God's law covenant with Israel, wherein he graciously leads them to Christ by showing them the perfect righteousness that only Christ could fulfill to redeem sinners.*

What Does the Bible Teach?

The fact that the Mosaic covenant is a covenant should require no defense. The explicit use of the word *covenant* for the relationship God created with Israel at Sinai is frequent. God himself calls it a covenant during the very drama at Sinai (see Ex. 19:5; 24:7–8; 34:10). As we discussed in the introduction, <u>a covenant is a relationship</u>, the <u>nature of the relationship being reflected in the covenant ceremony and details</u>. So the type of covenant God made with Israel at Sinai, revealed in its content, is the avenue to understanding the Mosaic.

Different from Abrahamic covenant. As we pointed out in the previous chapter, the data of Scripture show that the Mosaic covenant is a different covenant from the Abrahamic. This was in fact impressed deeply on the Israelite consciousness. In Deuteronomy 5:2–3, Moses says, "The LORD our God made a covenant with us in Horeb. Not with our fathers did the LORD make this covenant, but with us, who are all of us here alive today." Horeb is another name for Sinai. The phrase "our fathers" refers to the patriarchs in Deuteronomy, often found as "your/our fathers Abraham, Isaac and Jacob" (see Deut. 6:10; 9:5; 29:13). Therefore, Moses states that the covenant made at Sinai is different from the covenant God made with Abraham. The patriarchs are not part of the Sinai covenant, but Israel is. This is consonant with Paul's identification of the Abrahamic covenant as promise and the Mosaic as law instituted 430 years later (Gal. 3:17–19).

The difference is also felt in kind. In the Abrahamic covenant, God made a unilateral and gracious promise to Abraham, but to the nation of Israel God covenanted himself by works. Therefore, when Israel calls out to God for mercy and deliverance,

---

Gillespie, *The Ark of the Testament Opened* (London, 1661), 155; John Owen, *An Exposition of the Epistle to the Hebrews* in *Works* (Edinburgh: Banner of Truth, repr.1991), 22:70–78; Francis Turretin, *Institutes of Elenctic Theology* (Phillipsburg: P & R, 1994), 2:227–34; Herman Witsius, *The Economy of the Covenants between God & Man* (1693, Escondido: The den Dulk Foundation, 1990), 2:186.

they always appeal to Abraham and not to Moses (later on the Davidic promise will also be appealed to). An example of this is found in Deuteronomy 4, where God tells Israel that they will break his covenant and he will send them into exile. But in exile, God will redeem Israel for the sake of the oath given to Abraham (Deut. 4:25–31). Hence, through the rest of the Old Testament, Israel appeals to Abraham and not to Moses for mercy. As Calvin says, "But both Jeremiah and Paul, because they are contrasting the Old and New Testaments, consider nothing in the law except what properly belongs to it. For example: the law contains here and there promises of mercy, but because they have been borrowed from elsewhere, they are not counted part of the law, when only the nature of the law is under discussion."[4] Mercy does not properly belong to the Mosaic law. This does not mean God doesn't show mercy to Israel under Moses, for certainly he does, but this mercy does not come from the law of Moses. As Samuel Bolton, a member of the Westminster Assembly, said, the Mosaic was a covenant totally subservient to the covenant of grace. It was "temporary, and had respect to Canaan and God's blessing there, in obedience to it, and not to heaven, for that was promised by another Covenant which God made with [Israel] before He entered this."[5] The Abrahamic covenant, not the Mosaic, is the source of God's covenantal mercy to Israel.

So the Abrahamic and the Mosaic covenants are different. The patriarchs belong only to the Abrahamic. Israel, however, is in both. God redeemed Israel from Egypt and he gave them the land of Palestine graciously in keeping with his promise to the patriarchs (see Ex. 2:24; Deut. 9:5). The Abrahamic promises are fulfilled in Christ, so Israel is saved through faith in Christ, but these promises are administered and furthered through the Mosaic covenant, which is law, based on one's obedience to the terms.

Law Form. How then is the Mosaic covenant a covenant of law? As we saw in chapter 5, God's covenant with Abraham was gracious; its accommodated form was one of unilateral grant, where the promise was not dependent on Abraham's obedience. The accommodated form of the Mosaic, however, is one of

---

4. Calvin, *Institutes*, 2.11.7
5. Bolton, *True Bounds*, 145.

international treaty. Similar to today, the countries and nations of the ancient Near East had foreign policies and relations. They traded with one another, fought one another, and made peace. The agreements between the two nations were called covenants, which can be also called treaties to specify the type of covenant. These treaties had a fairly standardized form, as one would expect in such a formal and important relationship.

Nevertheless, such treaties often had terms. The treaty put the parties in a relationship that was defined by and dependent on the terms. If two countries make a peace treaty, then their peaceful relationship lasts only as long as both parties keep the terms. If the terms are broken, the nations become enemies once more. The relationship is defined by the terms of the agreement.

Similarly, God's covenant with Israel on Sinai had terms on which the covenant rested. As long as the terms are kept, the covenant lasts. But if the terms are violated, the covenant is broken and needs to be renewed or replaced with a new covenant. God is very clear that the blessings he promises to Israel are based on Israel's obedience to his law. God will give Israel long and blessed life in the Promised Land if they obey, but he will curse them with exile if they disobey.

This nature of the Mosaic covenant leaps off the page as soon as Israel reaches Sinai. In Exodus 19, Israel encamps at the foot of Sinai, and Moses goes up the mountain to receive God's word:

> Thus you shall say to the house of Jacob, and tell the people of Israel: You yourselves have seen what I did to the Egyptians, and how I bore you on eagles' wings and brought you to myself. Now therefore, if you will indeed obey my voice and keep my covenant, you shall be my treasured possession among all peoples, for all the earth is mine; and you shall be to me a kingdom of priests and a holy nation. These are the words that you shall speak to the people of Israel (vv. 3–6).

This is God's word that creates the Mosaic covenant and encapsulates the Mosaic theocracy. The divine commitment is that Israel will be a treasured possession to the Lord out of all the peoples. God promises to make his people a kingdom of priests and a holy nation. This promise is God's oath. The covenant formula can be sensed in this passage as God declares that he brought Israel to himself and that they will be his possession.

However, God promises to do this to Israel only if they very carefully obey his voice and keep his covenant. God's promise is conditioned on Israel's performance. If Israel does not obey, God is not obligated to bless them. This is like telling your daughter that she will only get dessert if she cleans her plate. Israel's status as God's possession is conditioned on their obedience. The covenant relationship is based on stipulations.

Covenants, further, had ratification ceremonies where oaths were taken and which dramatized the relationship. <u>The ratification ceremony for the Mosaic covenant is narrated for us in Exodus 24, which immediately precedes Exodus 19 historically.</u> Like Genesis 15, this ceremony illumines the relationship. At the foot of Sinai, the ceremony begins with Moses reading the words and statutes of the covenant. If one is to take an honest oath, he must know that to which he is swearing. The reading of the stipulations is followed by the Israelites promising, "All the words that the Lord has spoken we will do." They rightly swear fealty and obedience to the Lord. <u>Next, Moses builds an altar, representing the Lord, and twelve pillars to represent the twelve tribes</u> (v. 4). The blood of the sacrifices is collected into basins; <u>the blood is symbolic of the life-and-death consequences of the oath.</u> Then note what Moses does with the blood. He takes half of it and throws it against the altar; <u>he symbolically puts half of it on the Lord, which certifies the Lord's oath to Israel.</u> Like God passing through the carcasses in Genesis 15, this blood on the altar shows Israel that God will keep his oath of the covenant.

<u>The other half of the blood Moses throws on the people.</u> We should not visualize here Moses sprinkling blood over the heads of the crowds; rather, <u>Moses sprinkles the blood on the twelve stone pillars, which represent the people.</u> After Moses reads the whole book of the covenant and the people swear obedience in verse 7, Moses sprinkles the people with blood. At the foot of Sinai, both the altar and the twelve pillars are splattered with blood. This dramatically symbolized that both parties, the Lord and Israel, have passed through the carcasses and taken oaths. A covenant has been cut. Thus, Moses declares in verse 8, "Behold, the blood of the covenant

that the Lord has cut with you all" (my translation). Finally, the ceremony concludes with a covenant meal as Moses, Aaron, and the seventy elder-representatives of the people eat and drink with God on the mountain (vv. 9–11).

This ceremony demonstrates that the relationship is dependent on the oaths to performance by both parties. If God doesn't keep his word, the covenant is broken, which will of course never happen. If Israel doesn't keep their oath, the covenant is also broken. The relationship is based on works, and the consequence for failure is death.

The other place where the law-character of the Mosaic covenant is especially easy to see is in Deuteronomy. The nearly-omnipresent refrain in Deuteronomy is that Israel must be careful to keep the laws by doing them so that they may live long in the land. This refrain, burdensome by its incessant repetition, underscores the conditionality of the covenant. Blessings are earned by Israel's obedience, and curses for their disobedience. Moses summarizes this powerfully in 11:26–28, "See, I am setting before you today a blessing and a curse: the blessing, if you obey the commandments of the LORD your God, which I command you today, and the curse, if you do not obey the commandments of the LORD your God, but turn aside from the way that I am commanding you today." Israel's standing before God as either blessed or cursed rested on their keeping of the law. Israel would earn all sorts of blessings for obedience, and they would merit curses for disobedience (see Deut. 11:13–17). The people's law-keeping was their merit or righteousness before the Lord (Deut. 6:25). The law was the means whereby Israel remained in God's presence and favor.

The prophets further highlight this works-character of the Mosaic covenant. They declare that Israel is judged by the curses of the covenant for their disobedience, and they call the people to return to the Lord in obedience to receive favor and blessing. Isaiah's parable in 5:1–7 reflects the legal character of the Mosaic covenant. The Lord compares his people to a vineyard he planted, but when the Lord goes to look for fruit, he finds none; hence, the Lord is going to destroy the vineyard: "For the vineyard of the LORD of hosts is the house of Israel, and the men of Judah are his pleasant planting; and he looked for justice, but behold, bloodshed; for righteousness, but behold, an outcry!" (v. 7). The Mosaic covenant is compared to a business deal where one party did not uphold his part, so the unprofitable servant is fired.

Similarly the metaphor of divorce reflects the law foundation of Moses. Both Isaiah and Jeremiah compare the exile to a certificate of divorce that the Lord gave his wife because of her adulteries (Isa. 50:1; Jer. 3:8). Israel's idolatries are labeled sexual immorality and fornications. She violated her marriage with the Lord, and so he legally divorced her and sent her away. So, the Lord compared his relationship with Israel to Hosea and Gomer, where Gomer deserves to be stripped naked and to die of thirst in the desert (Hos. 2:3).

This works-character of the Mosaic covenant is why some Reformed theologians have labeled it as a republication of the original covenant of works. As John Owen concluded about the Mosaic covenant, "Now this is no other but the covenant of works revived."[6] Just as Adam had to obey to earn the reward of the covenant, so Israel had to keep the law to earn the blessings of the covenant. Obedience to the law was the means whereby they both obtained the reward.

This idea of republication highlights two things. First, it shows the basic continuity of God's law. The law God revealed on Sinai is fundamentally the same law Adam had to keep. So the Westminster Confession says about the law God gave to Adam, "This law, after his fall, continued to be a perfect rule of righteousness; and, as such, was delivered by God upon Mount Sinai, in the ten commandments" (WCF 19.2). Secondly, the doctrine of republication highlights the similar function that law had, namely to earn the reward. Both Adam and Israel earned the blessing by works of obedience.

Nevertheless, there is also a key difference. Whereas Adam could obey for eternal life, Israel was only to earn an earthly picture of heaven, the Promised Land. Israel was not saved by law.

Means to Holiness. Evidence in vast amounts could be amassed that demonstrate how Israel received blessing or curses based on

---

6. Owen, *Works*, 22:78. Sinai "revived, declared, and expressed *all the commands of that covenant in the decalogue* [sic]; for that is nothing but a divine summary of the law written in the heart of man at his creation." Like the covenant of works, the Mosaic covenant required perfect obedience, threatening death upon failure but eternal life upon fulfillment. "Yea, in sundry things it re-enforced, established, and confirmed that covenant." See *Works*, 22:70–78.

her obedience or disobedience. On virtually every page of the Law, the Historical Books and the Prophets, the Lord reminds Israel that she must obey or she will be judged and cursed. Nonetheless, to understand why God puts Israel in this law covenant, it is imperative to see how it symbolizes salvation. The Mosaic covenant and economy points to Christ and to heaven.

Under Moses, Israel became God's special people, who lived in his presence. The Promised Land was a holy land because it was the place of God's presence. Israel living in the Promised Land was their communing and living with God. Therefore, since the Lord is holy, Israel must be holy (Lev. 11:44–45), and Israel must attain this holiness by keeping the whole law; even the dietary laws were necessary in this. Indeed, the context of the command to be holy in Leviticus 11 is the dietary laws: "Be holy, for I am holy. You shall not defile yourselves with any swarming thing that crawls on the ground." Likewise, blood shed in wrongful killings polluted the holy land: "You shall not defile the land in which you live, in the midst of which I dwell, for I the LORD dwell in the midst of the people of Israel" (Num. 35:34).

Moreover, the command for Israel to destroy totally the Canaanites in the Promised Land is a purging of impurity, of anything other than what God had designated as holy. This is why the terms of warfare differed inside and outside the land. Deuteronomy 20 specifies that outside the Promised Land Israel can take plunder, slaves, wives, and even make peace; but inside the land, everything must be devoted to complete destruction as a whole burnt offering to the Lord (vv. 10–18).

The paradise-like blessings of the Mosaic covenant also reflect the beatitude of holiness. The blessings God promises Israel for obedience have an "other-worldly" character to them. For obedience, God promises that Israel will have no disease or barren women and cattle (Deut. 7:14–15), the land will be full of every good thing (Deut. 8:7–10), he will send rain (Deut. 11:13–15), there will be no more poor or needy among them (Deut. 15:4–5), they will have no enemies (Deut. 28:7), and they will be a lending bank to other nations but not borrow themselves (Deut. 28:12). Israel will be rich and free of hardship and enemies; no predators will harm their flocks; they will have large healthy families and flocks, and reside under the everlasting arms of God (Deut. 33:27–29).

All these holy and blessed aspects of the Mosaic covenant point to heaven and our ultimate salvation (Heb. 11:9–10). In the New Jerusalem, God's people will be glorified to reflect God's holiness, and no unclean thing will enter that holy place (Rev. 21:27). In glory, there will be no disease, poverty, or adversary, and we will lack no good thing. We will live in God's intimate presence in righteousness. The land of God's presence flowing with milk and honey was an earthly picture of the goal of ultimate salvation.

However, the crucial aspect of the Mosaic covenant is how Israel is to attain this earthly picture. What is the means whereby Israel stays in God's presence, dwells in his holy land, and enjoys his favor? Under Moses, it is by obedience to the law. The law was the means whereby Israel became and remained holy. Hence, the law is summarized in the words, "Do this and you will live" (Lev. 18:5). Israel's living in the land with God depends on their doing. Their righteous doing means blessed life in the holy land, while their wicked doing means the curse and wrath of God.

The uniqueness of the Mosaic is not that obedience is important for God's people. This has been and always will be the case, before Moses, now in the church age, and in glory. Rather, what is unique is the role of obedience to the law. Obedience to the law did not earn them heavenly salvation, but it did earn physical life in the land, the picture of heaven. The law was the means whereby Israel had physical life in God's presence. Thus, the Mosaic covenant is a test for Israel as an example for all of humanity. Could they obey the law to stay in God's presence, to have communion with him? The Mosaic covenant is like the son's time in the garage alone with the Mustang. The father is teaching his son the lesson that he can't do it alone. Hence, the Mosaic covenant was temporary from the beginning.

This probationary character of the Mosaic covenant is also clear from the curse of the covenant. What is its ultimate curse? It is not death but being forsaken by God. The curses of Deuteronomy 28, which begin in verse 15 of that long chapter, do not end with the extinction of Israel. Instead, the curses end with the Exodus being undone; they are back in exile begging others to buy them as slaves (v. 68). Reading about the plagues, the war, and mothers eating their children in the siege, you feel the people have died a thousand deaths. It is amazing that any Israelites survive, but they do so only to plead for someone to buy them as slaves in Egypt, where the Mosaic covenant began. Likewise, the curses in Leviticus 26 conclude with Israel rotting away in the land of their enemies (v. 38–39). Hosea prophesies that they will go back to Egypt and away to Assyria (8:9–14), which is precisely what happens in 2 Kings 17:7–23.

Counterbalancing the blessing, the curse is a picture of hell, which is not non-existence but the weeping and gnashing of teeth because of being forsaken. Can you imagine begging someone to buy you as a slave? Is this not a picture of being without God and without hope in the world, which is where the Gentiles are before Christ (Eph. 2:12)? In fact, this is covenantal context for Jesus' cry on the cross, "My God, my God, why have you forsaken me?" (Matt. 27:46). Israel failed to obey the terms of the Mosaic covenant, and they were cursed in exile, a picture of the God-forsakenness of hell.

Destined to Fail. Nevertheless, this failure of Israel to stay in God's presence by means of obeying the law was preached to Israel from the beginning. In Deuteronomy 4, Moses says to those standing on the plains of Moab, "I call heaven and earth to witness against you today, that you will soon utterly perish from the land that you are going over the Jordan to possess. You will not live long in it, but will be utterly destroyed. And the LORD will scatter you among the peoples, and you will be left few in number among the nations where the LORD will drive you" (vv. 26–27). In Deuteronomy 30:1, the Lord declares, "When all these things come upon you, the blessing and the curse, which I have set before you." So also, Israel's national anthem found in Deuteronomy 32 testifies that Israel will grow fat in her sin and be exiled. God told Israel from the start that they would fail. As a nation, they would not be able to obey the law as the means to stay in his presence.

Consider the effect of this on the faith of the Israelites. God makes a covenant with you where you have to obey his law perfectly as a corporate nation to be with him in the blessed and holy land, all of which is a good thing. Who wouldn't want such earthly blessings? Then God tells you that you are going to fail. The curses will come upon the holy nation. This might not happen in your lifetime, but it will happen. How does this make you feel? It should make you realize that you cannot earn God's eternal favor by your obedience; no man can be justified by the works of the law. Instead, you must put your faith in God to provide the necessary righteousness on your behalf.

Israel's inevitable failure drove them to look for a Mediator, for God also promised Israel a newer and greater life after he exiled them (Deut. 30:1–4; Lev. 26:40–45). Their failure was for their ultimate good, even if they did not always grasp it. Hence, the destined failure of Israel made the law-covenant of Moses one of perpetual renewal. In ancient treaties, the lesser king had to renew his vows to the greater king on a regular basis. The treaty was reread, possibly updated and altered, and the lesser king again swore loyalty to his covenant superior and lord. If the inferior party had violated the terms, this was especially the case. The great king would punish his vassal and remake the covenant, unless the vassal was completely destroyed. Likewise, Israel's sin was a violation of the covenant, making it necessary that it be renewed. This renewal of the covenant is found throughout Israel's history and is even built into the ceremonial system of the Mosaic covenant.

The historical renewals came when Israel grievously rebelled against God, and it did not take long for this to happen. Indeed, after the golden calf episode in Exodus 32, God is ready to wipe Israel off the face of the earth completely (vv. 7–10). The shattering of the covenant tablets symbolizes the breaking of the covenant (32:19). Yet, for the sake of his oath to Abraham, God shows mercy to Israel and renews the covenant with new tablets (Ex. 34:10–28). Other historical renewals are narrated through the Old Testament. The book of Deuteronomy is a covenant renewal on the plains of Moab before Israel crosses the Jordan. Joshua renews the Sinai covenant in Joshua 24. Solomon's dedication of the temple functions as a renewal (1 Kings 8). The covenant is renewed again under Jehoiada (2 Kings 11:17–20), Josiah (2 Kings 22–23), and Nehemiah (Neh. 9).

Besides these major historical renewals, the Lord built renewals into the ceremonial system of Sinai, most formally in the Day of Atonement. On the tenth day of the seventh month, the high priest was to go into the Holy of Holies to make atonement for all of Israel's sins. Israel had to remain holy to stay in God's holy land, but they were sinners and creators of impurity, which deserved the curses. So the Lord gave them a feast to purify themselves every year for a fresh start. This renewal aspect was not limited only to the Day of Atonement. Renewals could be included in other feasts like Passover (Josh. 5, Josiah in 2 Kings 23) or the Feast of Weeks (called Pentecost in New Testament) (2 Chron. 15:10–15). <u>Furthermore, every seventh year at the Feast of Booths the whole Torah was to be reread in the hearing of all the people, which is a typical part of the covenant renewal ceremony</u> (Deut. 31:9–13).

This perpetual renewal of the Mosaic covenant demonstrates two things. First, the need for renewal shows the covenant relationship was based on works of obedience and oaths of loyalty. Israel's failure meant the relationship was not in a state of well-being, so it had to be renewed, and Israel had to be purified again. Second, the institution of these renewals demonstrates the Lord's larger purposes of grace. If ultimate salvation depended on their works, the Lord would have destroyed Israel completely the first time they broke the covenant, and it would all have been finished (as God was tempted to do in Exodus 32). <u>Instead, the Lord builds in renewals because his overall purpose is to lead his people to Christ, which would never happen without renewals.</u> The Sovereign had the authority and right to destroy his covenant-breaking partner. The Lord's patience and longsuffering with Israel shows that the Mosaic covenant is a strict pedagogue leading to Jesus, serving God's gracious purposes.

Why Is This Doctrine Important for the Christian Life?

These broad strokes of the Mosaic covenant show how God drove Israel, and drives us, to Christ for salvation. God's justice requires that heaven be earned by perfect obedience to his law. This is what Christ came to do as our covenantal representative. He obeyed the law in our stead so that by faith we can become the righteousness of God in him (2 Cor. 5:21). Christ earned the glory of heaven for his people, which we receive as a gift through faith. As we learned in chapter 1, this is what the Father and Son agreed to in the covenant of redemption. This is yet another reason why the Mosaic covenant was necessary. It provided Christ with the temporal and historical setting to obtain eternal life for those whom he represented in the covenant of redemption. As the Puritan Samuel Petto (c. 1624–1711) noted,

> The Covenant of Works being broken by us in the first Adam, it was of great concernment to us, that satisfaction should be given to it, for unless its righteousness were performed for us, the Promised Life was unattainable; and unless its penalty were undergone for us, the threatened Death (Gen. 2.17) was unavoidable.[7]

Sinai gave the Son the opportunity to perform, through his active and passive obedience, the righteousness that the original covenant of works required. This made the Mosaic covenant a necessary and vital part of God's plan of redemption:

> If he had not been born under the very Law, as a Covenant of Works, he should not have satisfied it, by answering the penalty or fulfilling the righteousness of it, but had only done and suffered something in lieu and stead thereof, it would not have been the *idem* for us; and this sheweth how exceedingly necessary the Sinai Covenant was.[8]

Born under the Mosaic Law with a real body and soul, Christ was able to fulfill what he promised in the covenant of redemption and earn for himself and the Father a people and everlasting glory. Thus, God is both just and the justifier of the ungodly in Christ through faith (Rom. 3:26; 4:5).

Our problem as fallen humans, however, is to think we do not really need Christ. We can obey God's law enough. God is not really that holy or just. We are not such bad sinners. Hence, God gave us Israel, who was also his son (Deut. 1:31; Hos. 11:1). God put Israel in a temporary law-covenant, wherein Israel had to earn the earthly picture of heaven by her works. In the Mosaic law, God revealed the perfect righteousness his justice required (Rom. 3:21). God's holiness burned brightly, like the pillar of fire at Sinai, consuming everyone who touched the mountain.

God demanded of his son Israel obedience to his law to merit the blessings of the covenant. If Israel could earn the earthly blessings

---

7. Samuel Petto, *The Difference Between the Old and New Covenants* (London, 1674), 125.
8. Petto, 135–6.

by their obedience, then there might be a chance for fallen man to earn his way to heaven. Yet, generation after generation, Israel failed miserably. Israel was barely off the shores of the Red Sea when Aaron made the golden calf. In Judges, each generation intermarried with the Canaanites and worshiped their gods. Despite all his wisdom and riches, Solomon lusted after the gods of his many wives. Then every king, one after another, kept sinning against the Lord. Some were better than others, but none of them could prevent the curses of the covenant from coming. Israel could not stay in God's presence by means of the law. They could not earn life with God. Even after such a powerful lesson as the exile, Jesus comes to find Israel led by a brood of vipers, where even the teachers of the law are whitewashed tombs. Without a doubt, the Mosaic covenant paints across history in the lives of real people that no man can be justified by works of the law; rather, none is righteous. All have turned aside; no one does good, not even one.

Do you think you can in some way, ever so small, earn something from God? Well, look at Israel and think again. Even the impressive piety of Moses and David is not good enough. Moses struck the rock and died outside the Promised Land. David slept with Bathsheba and commanded the census and was punished. As the fallen children of Adam, we need to become the righteousness of God to have everlasting life in heaven with God, but there is no way we can do this ourselves, even with help. Rather, we need one to do it all for us, and this we find in Jesus Christ. He is the Righteous One, who was born under the law and of a woman. He is the true Israel who remained obedient to death, even death on a cross.

The Mosaic covenant powerfully points us to Christ precisely due to its strictness. He is the One who fulfilled Sinai's command, "Do this and live" (Lev. 18:5). The moment we begin to water down the law character of this covenant, the work of Christ starts to become obscured. If we are blind to the depth of our sin, then we are handicapped in perceiving the grace of God to save us in Christ. As the saying goes, if you don't understand sin, you will never understand grace. So God gives us the history of Israel to show us our sinful identity. We discover our spiritual poverty, not primarily through introspection, but by looking to the revelation of God in history as he deals with his people. As Paul remarks about the Old Testament history, "Now, these things happened to them as types and were written down for our instruction" (1 Cor. 10:11, my translation). By types, Paul means that the events Israel experienced were pictures or models of things to come. They pictured not only Christ but also us. This fact reveals that the law is still the guide for our life in pleasing God, as the Psalmist says, "Your word is a lamp to my feet and a light to my path" (Ps. 119:105).

The Mosaic covenant, then, lays the historical and covenantal context for Christ. Jesus was born of a woman and under the law (Gal. 4:4). Jesus Christ comes as the true Son of God, who is able to obey perfectly the law as the kingly representative of his people, and he thereby earns not the earthly picture but the heavenly reality. Jesus makes true atonement once for all by his blood, and he provides the necessary righteousness for us, which we receive through faith alone.

Moreover, Israel's constant failure under Moses shows us that we need Christ just as they did. The strictness of the Mosaic covenant reminds us that we have no hope of salvation outside of Christ. Obedience for everlasting life is impossible for mankind, but with God it is possible, for he provided Christ. And this is a true help to our faith. As we go about our everyday lives, it is easy for us to think little of Christ and for our self-confidence before God to depend on our daily performance. We suppose that if we had a good day, God loves us; but if we had a bad day, God does not love us. Yet our standing before God depends on Christ alone. By his righteousness we are justified. By his grace we are sanctified. By his love we can love in return. By his faithfulness we are brought to our heavenly home.

Questions for Further Reflection

1. How does Exodus 24 show that the Mosaic covenant is based on works?
2. How does the Mosaic covenant picture the doctrine of salvation?
3. Why is holiness so important under the Mosaic covenant?

4. How is the Mosaic covenant similar to and different from the original covenant of works?

5. How does the strict law-character of the Mosaic covenant shed light on the work of Christ?

6. Explain how Israel's constant failures drive us to Christ.

7

The King Who Did:
THE DAVIDIC COVENANT

In America we have a peculiar estimation of kings and royalty. Politically, America is the country that threw off the tyrannical yoke of the king. The flag we fly displays the virtuous superiority of a democratic republic. In conversations on history, past monarchs tend to get censured as oppressive and despotic. We want nothing to do with kings in our everyday political life. Yet there is no shortage of kings in our various forms of amusement. Movies and books about kings and royal families are a common dish in our entertainment diet. These may be historical, fantasy, or futuristic. The king may be corrupt or noble, but we thoroughly enjoy stories about kings. Think of how many Americans tune in when there is a royal wedding in England. We are happy to have a sort of celebrity fascination with kings in the world of fiction and imagination, but we are adamant that they have no rightful place in the real world.

This peculiar attitude concerning kings makes it difficult for us to understand the ancient world, where monarchies dominated the landscape. Monarchs monopolized the world of ancient Israel. To be a people, you needed two things: a land and a ruler. Without a land, one was a wanderer, a vagabond. Without a ruler, one was exposed and unprotected, ready to be swallowed up by a foreign ruler. There is no question that these kings could be cruel and oppressive, but often they were relatively just and virtuous. Kings could be a curse for the people, but they could also be a tremendous blessing. One of the primary duties of the king was to provide peace and protection for the people. Kings took titles and duties of father and shepherd to the people. Kings regularly helped the poor and needy of society. They would forgive debts and grant certain groups immunity to taxes. The king was a significant part of the subject's life. Typically, the better things were for the king, the better they were for you.

This was the world of Israel and David. These were the virtues and conceptions of kingship that God used to speak of the office that Christ fulfilled as our king. As modern Americans, then, we need to set aside some of our cultural antipathy for kings so we may better grasp how Christ is our King. In fact, we can use some of our imaginative fascination with royalty to transport us back into the world of Scripture. For when we do, we realize that the Davidic covenant is the regal glory crowning all the other Old Testament covenants; and so, it showcases with greater clarity the person and work of Christ for us, past, present, and future.

What Is the Davidic Covenant?

Before we turn to specific Scripture texts to tease out the beauty of kingship, it is necessary to set forth a working definition of the Davidic covenant. We are no strangers to David, as he may be the best known person in Scripture. The books of 1 and 2 Samuel trace his life from a young boy to his death as an old man. As children, one of the first Bible stories we learned was the story of David and Goliath. The Psalms, of which David is the principle author, play such a dear place in our daily devotions and worship in the church. We sing, memorize, and pray the Psalms David wrote. And some of the Psalms are so personal in character, such as Psalm 51, where he confesses his sin with Bathsheba. The Psalms bring us into David's private prayer closet. Who else in Scripture do we know so well? And who could be better than the one called, "a man after God's own heart"?

And yet, even though we know David the man so well, we do not seem to be nearly as familiar with David as king. Our knowledge of David the man does not translate as easily into appreciation for his kingship. However, Scripture only presents David to us as king. The very first time we are introduced to David in 1 Samuel 16 is when Samuel has gone to Bethlehem to anoint a king. We know nothing of David until two verses before he is anointed (1 Sam. 16:11–13). We know little of his life before his anointing, only that he was a shepherd, the youngest of eight boys. There is no birth narrative of David and no prophetic portent about him to his mother or father. David does not come on the scene until the anointing oil is poured on his head. This means that everything we know about David, we know about him *as king*. One could say Scripture has no interest in David outside of his being king. All the personal and intimate knowledge we have of David is given so that we might know him as king, so that we might better grasp the office of king in God's plan of redemption in Christ.

The Davidic covenant is God's promise to David that secures and seals his kingship. This covenant is what guarantees that David's kingship will play the pivotal role in God's work of redeeming his people. If it were not for the Davidic covenant, David's kingship would have come and gone. God would have chosen another dynasty through which to work his redemption. Kingship would still have played a role in God's plan, but it would not have been David's kingship without this covenant.

So the Davidic covenant can be defined as <u>God's promise to David that, when his righteous Son builds a house for God's name, God will grant him an eternal kingdom.</u>

What Does the Bible Teach?

2 Samuel 7. This passage is the genesis of the Davidic covenant (along with its parallel in 1 Chronicles 17). It is the fountainhead from which course all the deep biblical waters concerning David, kingship, and Christ. It is also a dense and rich passage, which means we need to spend some time unpacking its capital. Before we walk through the passage, a few remarks to set the stage are necessary.

<u>First, this passage is another example of how Scripture can present a covenant without using the word.</u> The word *covenant* is not used once in this chapter or its surrounding chapters. Yet this promise of God to David is clearly a covenant. David himself acknowledges this

fact as he reflects on what God did for him in his last words: "[God] has made with me an everlasting covenant" (2 Sam. 23:5). This is also brought out in numerous other passages of Scripture (2 Chron. 13:5; 21:7; Isa. 55:3; Ps. 89:3; 132:11; 2 Kings 8:19). To cite just one of the clearest passages, the Lord said in Jeremiah 33:20–21, "If you can break my covenant with the day and my covenant with the night . . . then also my covenant with David my servant may be broken, so that he shall not have a son to reign on his throne." This passage is helpful because it calls God's promise to David a "covenant" and because it also uses the language of 2 Samuel 7 about a son on David's throne.

Second, the context of 1 and 2 Samuel has led us to this chapter. So far, David has shown himself above reproach and truly a man after God's own heart, especially in contrast to the ever-increasing wickedness of Saul. This contrast between David and Saul was set up for us way back in 1 Samuel 13:13–14 when Samuel rebuked Saul:

> You have done foolishly. You have not kept the command of the LORD your God, with which he commanded you. For then the LORD would have established your kingdom over Israel forever. But now your kingdom shall not continue. The LORD has sought out a man after his own heart, and the LORD has commanded him to be prince over his people, because you have not kept what the LORD commanded you.

Unlike Saul, David proved himself upright and devoted to the Lord. Therefore, in 2 Samuel 5, David is finally made king over all Israel, and he strikes the Philistines a final blow. Next, as one of David's first acts as king, he brings up the ark to Jerusalem. David reveals his concern for the Lord as the primary task of his kingship. This brings us to 2 Samuel 7, where David is living in his house, or palace, having rest from all his surrounding enemies.

Third, there is a significant word play that runs through this chapter, especially verses 1–17. This play is on the word *house*. In Hebrew, *house* can refer to several things. In terms of a dwelling, it can refer to a house, palace, or temple. In terms of family, it can mean a household, a family line, or a dynasty. *House* can also include a nation, a people, or a kingdom, so the house of Israel is the people or kingdom of Israel. Well, in 2 Samuel 7, there are three main uses for *house*: temple, dynasty, and people/kingdom. The Lord plays off these to reveal the brilliant message about his dwelling place and the role of the king. The play off *house* really shapes the contours of God's promise to David.

At the opening of 2 Samuel 7, David is reclining in his cedar palace, having rest from all his enemies (v. 1). But as he looks down from this cedar balcony, he notices that the ark of God is in a tent. This discrepancy troubles David deeply. His kingship is to be first and foremost religious, for God. David desires to honor God with a glorious cedar house as well, and Nathan advises him to do what is in his heart. The Lord, however, appears to Nathan that night to put the brakes on David's temple-building plans.

The Lord puts the question to David, "Would you build me a house to dwell in?" (v. 5). This brings up the issue of whether God has ever asked for a house of cedar and what kind of house in which God desires to reside. As God notes, he has never asked any of the judges before David to build him a house, that is a temple (v. 7), but he has been contented with being in a Tent. Yet the Lord hints that his residence is not limited to the Tent. There are two parallel phrases here: "I have been moving about in a tent" (v. 6); "I have been moving about with all the people of Israel" (v. 7). It is not merely the Tent that is God's dwelling, but it is the Tent with the people. Already, God has linked together a structure (tent or temple) and the people in the understanding of his house.

This, though, amounts to God telling David, "No, you cannot build me a house" (explicitly stated in 1 Chron. 17:4). Instead of David building for God, God will act for David. Just as God has been with David, so now God will make David's name great, appoint a place for his people, and give him rest from all enemies (vv. 9–11). The climactic promise comes in verse 11, "The LORD declares to you that the LORD will make you a house." David cannot build the Lord a house, but the Lord will build David a house. What sort of house is this? The Lord clarifies that he is referring to David's offspring (v. 12). This house is David's family line, but more specifically, "I will establish his kingdom." The house is David's dynasty—his kingly descendants.

Additionally, the Lord promises, "I will be to him a father, and he shall be to me a son." This is an adoption formula, which intensifies the intimacy between God and David's son. David is not called God's son, but David's offspring is God's son. This promise focuses the Davidic covenant less on David himself and more on David's son. And as a good father, the Lord declares that his steadfast love will be upon David's son, never to depart (v. 15). In fact, God assures David that his house and kingdom will be everlasting. Literally, "your enduring house and kingdom will be forever before me" (v. 16, my translation). David's house, his dynastic lineage, is connected to his kingdom. For what is a kingdom without a king? The Lord, then, promises David a house, a kingdom, and a throne, upon which God's love will be established forever.

Unconditional Promise. The details of this promise reveal the first prong of the Davidic covenant, that it is unconditional and everlasting. It is God's gracious promise that cannot be broken. God's love will be upon David's son to establish his house, kingdom, and throne forever. As he was faithful in his promise to Abraham, God will surely fulfill his promise, and nothing can stop him. The unconditional and permanent nature of the Davidic covenant is made even more explicit by passages like Jeremiah 33:20–21 quoted above, where God states that it is impossible to break his covenant with David, just as it is impossible to break his covenant with day and night. In similar language, Psalm 89 lifts up as a glorious banner this unconditional aspect. The Lord states there, "I will not violate my covenant or alter the word that went forth from my lips. Once for all I have sworn by my holiness; I will not lie to David. His offspring shall endure forever, his throne as long as the sun before me. Like the moon it shall be established forever, a faithful witness in the skies" (vv. 34–37). This language could hardly be more lofty and stunning. For the Davidic covenant to be broken would be for God to lie, which cannot and never will happen.

The unconditional nature of the Davidic covenant furthermore orients it towards the future. It is not David that will be on this eternal throne but his son. The eternal establishment of David's house and kingdom lies in the future, though how far in the future is not clear from 2 Samuel 7. From God's words here, there is little reason for David to doubt that it would be fulfilled in his immediate son. The Lord told David he would raise up "your offspring, from your own body." Naturally, David would look to his son, which is confirmed by the narrative of 2 Samuel and 1 Chronicles. This expectation creates a first level of fulfillment of the Davidic covenant. In Solomon, it appears that God is fulfilling his promise to David, but with the failure of Solomon, the future horizon gets extended for the true fulfillment of the covenant, as we shall see shortly.

Conditional Element. There is, however, another prong to the Davidic covenant. The first prong is its fundamentally unconditional nature. The second prong entails a conditional element, where something is required of David's son. David's son must do something in order to receive the eternal throne. This conditional element does not take center stage in 2 Samuel 7, but it is not left out. In verse 13, the conditional element gets its air time: "He shall build a house for my name, and then I will establish the throne of his kingdom forever" (my translation). The Lord establishing his throne depends on the son's building of the house. David's son must do something to have his throne founded.

Here is where the play on *house* is most intriguing. Clearly, temple is at the fore. David's son must be the temple builder. David cannot build the temple as a man of war, but his son of peace must build the temple (1 Kings 5:3). Yet God's house implicitly includes the people (v. 7) and house has been linked to kingdom. The son's work then is not merely a construction project but also entails God's people and kingdom. Furthermore, the house David's son must build is "for my name" (v. 13). The house is for God's name, to honor and glorify him. This includes religious devotion and obedience. Obedience must color the son's work of building, which makes sense of God's discipline of the son in verse 14. When iniquity plays a role in the son's building, God will discipline and correct him as a father. The conditional element requires an obedient building of the son secured by the Father's discipline.

1 Kings 9. This conditional element of the unconditional Davidic covenant is, however, infantile in 2 Samuel 7; but as the narrative of 2 Samuel progresses into 1 Kings, it matures into adulthood, culminating in 1 Kings 9. Leading up to 1 Kings 9, we learn that Solomon is the chosen son of David to rule. David solidifies Solomon's succession and kingdom. Solomon rightly asks God for "an understanding mind to govern your people, that I may discern between good and evil" (1 Kings 3:9). Solomon's correct petition focused on obedient rule for God's sake.

After this, Solomon begins well. He rules with wisdom and justice, so that soon all the people, as numerous as the sand by the sea, are dwelling richly in peace, each man under his vine and under his fig tree (1 Kings 4:25). Solomon then finishes the temple of God with an opulence fitting God's glory. The ark is brought up to the temple, and God's glory fills it. And with all of these events, Solomon confirms that the Lord has fulfilled the promise to David in him: "Now the LORD has fulfilled his promise that he made. For I have risen in the place of David my father, and sit on the throne of Israel, as the LORD promised, and I have built the house for the name of the LORD, the God of Israel" (1 Kings 8:20). On the first level, the Davidic promises seem to have been fulfilled. Yet this first level is not the true fulfillment of the covenant, which is made clear from God's second appearance to Solomon in 1 Kings 9.

The Lord comes to Solomon again and assures him that He has heard Solomon's prayer. The Lord has consecrated the temple as holy and has made his name to dwell there (v. 3). He has approved of the temple, and it will be the place of worship for God's people. God then focuses on Solomon saying, "And as for you, if you will walk before me . . . doing according to all that I have commanded you, and keeping my statutes and my rules, then I will establish your royal throne over Israel forever, as I promised David" (vv. 4–5). In 1 Kings 8, Solomon thought he already deserved an eternal throne, but the Lord says, "Only if you obey." The Lord will only establish the throne of David's righteous son. Due to the unconditional nature of the covenant, a Davidic son will always be on the throne, but only the obedient son will get an everlasting throne.

This passage makes clear how the unconditional prong and conditional prong work together in the Davidic covenant. Because of God's unbreakable oath, the Davidic dynasty must continue. If the dynasty is erased from history, God has lied, which cannot be. It is, however, only the righteous son of David who will receive an eternal throne for his obedience. The future direction of the Davidic covenant is then mapped out. God will be true to his promise to David to sustain his dynasty. God will keep putting

David's sons on the throne; when the son is disobedient, God will remove that son and install another son. This pattern will continue until a righteous son is found to earn the everlasting throne, needing no more successors.

Furthermore, we cannot miss how this requirement for righteousness picks up the works-principle in Moses. The language of verse 4 about doing his commands, walking before him, and keeping God's statutes and rules is pulled right out of Deuteronomy. The Davidic son has to keep the law of Moses—this is the righteousness he must fulfill for an eternal throne. The Mosaic connection is also found if the son fails. In verses 6–9, if the Davidic son disobeys God and turns to idols, "then I will cut off Israel from the land" (v. 7). Again this is curse language for exile pulled from Deuteronomy, but note how the Lord says, if the king disobeys, then the people will be cut off. The curse of exile comes on the whole people for the king's disobedience. The works-principle of Moses has shifted from the whole people to the king. The reality of this culminates in the gross apostasy of Manasseh, about whom God says, "Because Manasseh king of Judah has committed these abominations . . . Behold, I am bringing upon Jerusalem and Judah such disaster that the ears of everyone who hears of it will tingle" (2 Kings 21:11–12).

The house the king must build is not just a temple, but it is an obedient people for God's name. The son of David, who is righteous and who makes the people righteous, is the one who will have his throne established forever. The conditional dynamic of the unconditional covenant becomes the map for the rest of biblical history. After Solomon's failure and death, God punishes the house of David by dividing the kingdom. Yet, in the southern kingdom of Judah, God's steadfast love to David continues.

Two patterns emerge in the following history. First, the piety of the king determines the piety of the people. If the king is obedient, so are the people; but if the king is disobedient, so are the people. Second, a refrain is found in each account of a king. Each successive Davidic son is compared to David, the man after God's heart. The assessment is sometimes positive ("He did what was right in the eyes of the Lord, as David his father did," 1 Kings 15:11); and other times it is negative ("His heart was not wholly true to the Lord his

God, as the heart of David his father," 1 Kings 15:3). Yet, when the king is disobedient, another line is added ("Nevertheless, for David's sake the Lord his God gave him a lamp in Jerusalem, setting up his son after him," 1 Kings 15:4). These refrains dot the following pages of biblical history. They demonstrate that the Lord's fatherly discipline of David's son removes the disobedient son but faithfully places another son on the throne. And the pattern will continue until that one truly righteous son arises. God will never break his covenant to the house of David, but it is only the righteous son of David who will gain that everlasting throne.

Psalm 2. Many passages could be mentioned to exhibit the nature of the Davidic covenant. But it is good to bring up a few briefly to display the fullness of the Davidic covenant, especially as it looks forward to Christ. Psalm 2 is an enthronement song, meaning it celebrates the inauguration of a new Davidic king. On this joyous occasion, note what God says of that son of David: "I have set my King on Zion, my holy hill" (v. 6). The kingship of God is married to the kingship of David's house. Then the Lord declares to the newly anointed king, "You are my son; today I have begotten you" (v. 7). Picking up from 2 Samuel 7, the Lord is a father to the king, and the king is God's son. Likewise, the begetting does not refer to the king being begotten in his mother's womb but his anointing as king—it is "today." "Son of God" or "God's son" becomes a title for the Davidic king. Finally, this Psalm is directed at the nations who rage, who are told to kiss the Son lest he be angry. The Davidic kingship is not only for Israel but it also has implications for the nations.

Psalm 16. Here David expresses confidence in the Lord's faithfulness and love to preserve him through trials. The primary trial is not enemies but death: "For you will not abandon my soul to Sheol, or let your holy one see corruption" (v. 10). The shift from "my soul" to "holy one" is crucial. This reveals that David's confidence for himself is not merely in the Lord not abandoning him to Sheol, but in the holy one not seeing corruption. It is David's holy and righteous son that will not see decay in the grave. Peter proves that Jesus is the Christ from this very Psalm. In Acts 2, Peter declares that, since David died, he cannot be the fulfillment of Psalm 16. But Jesus, who is now raised from the dead, must be. The resurrection of Jesus authenticates that Jesus is the holy and righteous son of David. A righteousness that conquers death is necessary for the Son of David to gain a truly *everlasting* throne.

Psalm 110. This Psalm of David is one of the most-often quoted Psalms in the New Testament to show the kingship of Christ. Much could be said about this Psalm, but several quick points are sufficient for our purposes. (1) The son of David's reign has a heavenly dimension to it, as God says to the king, "Sit at my right hand!" The right hand of God's throne is in heaven, which is Peter's point in Acts 2:33–34. (2) A priestly function is added to the Davidic kingship: "You are a priest forever after the order of Melchizedek" (v. 4). (3) David understood that his son would be greater than he: "The LORD says to *my* Lord" (emphasis added). Originally, David probably penned the psalm thinking of Solomon, and sons are not lords to their fathers. Yet David understood that the sonship of God that belonged to his son would make him his royal superior. This is Jesus' point in Matthew 22:41–46. (4) At God's right hand, David's Lord has to execute judgments among the nations (vv. 5–6). The Davidic King has to subdue the world for the sake of his holy people (1 Cor. 15:25).

The New Testament. The Davidic covenant is the great hope for Israel. Since it was secured by an everlasting promise that could not be broken, Israel knew that God would save them through the Davidic King. The Davidic King would make the people holy, establishing the true temple of God. He would keep the law for the people as their representative. The Son of David would subdue all Israel's enemies and would reign in God's name and holiness. The King would usher them into Zion to worship God forever in glory (Ps. 132:13–18). The reign of David's son would dawn on the people "like the morning light, like the sun shining forth on a cloudless morning, like rain that makes grass to sprout from the earth" (2 Sam. 23:4). And yet it was only the righteous son of David who could do this for Israel. Israel had to wait in faith for the true son of David. The Davidic covenant gave the house of Jacob assurance of God's salvation, but it called them to wait, to be patient for the greater and righteous Son of David.

Eagerly waiting is how we find Israel at the opening of the New Testament. There has not been a king of the Davidic throne for over five hundred years, since Nebuchadnezzar destroyed the temple in 586 BC. They wondered when the Lord would raise up the anointed son of David, the Christ or Messiah, to save them. In the words of Psalm 89, the people asked God, "Lord, where is your steadfast love of old, which by your faithfulness you swore to David?" (v. 49). And it was such an inquiry that the angel answered when he told Mary about her son, "He will be great and will be called the Son of the Most High. And the Lord God will give to him the throne of his father David, and he will reign over the house of Jacob forever, and of his kingdom there will be no end" (Luke 1:32–33). Jesus came as the greater son of David to fulfill the Davidic covenant by building a house for God's name.

The centrality of the Davidic covenant in the Old Testament is the reason why it so monopolizes the New Testament in describing the person and work of Christ. The very title of Christ or Messiah means *anointed one,* which referred to the anointed son of David. The Christ was king. When Jesus rides into Jerusalem on a foal in the triumphal entry, the people cry out that "your king is coming to you" (Matt. 21:5). Yet Jesus' humility was teaching the people that the king for whom they waited was bringing forth a different kind of kingdom from what they expected. As Jesus told Pilate, "My kingdom is not of this world. If my kingdom were of this world, my servants would have been fighting, that I might not be delivered over to the Jews. But my kingdom is not from the world" (John 18:36). Jesus brought forth a spiritual and heavenly kingdom. The house he built was not built with wood and stone but with living people. The spiritual house he built was the church (1 Cor. 6:19; Eph. 2:20–22; 1 Pet. 2:5).

As Peter proves that Jesus is both Christ and Lord in his great Pentecost sermon, he argues from the Davidic covenant (Acts 2:22–36). In Peter's sermon of Acts 3, he uses the title "Holy and Righteous One" for Jesus whom the people denied (3:14). This title refers to the righteous son of David for whom the people were waiting. Paul also turns to the Davidic covenant to show that Jesus' resurrection means he is God's true Son, through whom we have forgiveness of sins (Acts 13:32–39). Therefore, the Davidic covenant is like a microscope that allows us to zoom in and see all the beautiful shades and glorious lines of Christ's work as King for us.

Why Is This Doctrine Important for the Christian Life?

From the previous discussion it should be clear that the spiritual benefit of the Davidic covenant can hardly be overemphasized. The person and work of Christ cannot be properly or fully grasped without the Davidic covenant. Jesus' work of salvation is left without a context if the Davidic covenant is not understood. As God's pilgrim people, we constantly need to hear the assurance of the gospel. The firmness of the gospel is further solidified by the Davidic covenant. This promise of God was established forever like the moon in the skies (Psalm 89:37). The only way for the Davidic covenant to be broken is for God to lie, which can never happen. God's promise to David just awaited that Righteous Heir, and Jesus Christ is he!

Born of the Virgin Mary, of the line of David, as God's true Son, holy and blameless, Christ came as the temple builder for God's name. And he constructed the only temple God can ever live in, a spiritual temple where God's people are the living stones and are holy. Christ Jesus did this by his blood. He imputed his righteousness to us, and his blood purged away all our sins to make us the temple of the living God. So in Revelation 21:3, when the Lord says, "Behold, the dwelling place of God is with man," this is true because Christ fulfilled the Davidic covenant.

Besides undergirding the gospel, the Davidic covenant also guarantees our blessed hope for us. As Hebrews says, we do not presently see everything in subjection to him (Heb. 2:8). Not all the enemies are under Christ's kingly feet. We know this all too well, do we not? The sin, evil, and death of this world are all around us. In our country, we are not under a king. There are many benefits to the checks and balances of a democratic republic. Yet things are hardly fine. Corruption is still rampant. Tax dollars are wasted. The courts struggle to punish obvious criminals, besides the fact that many of our laws are far from upright. And on top of this, death still runs around wild. Yet it is not just in the world that evil is prevalent. False teaching, schism, and sin plague the church. The visible church as the earthly expression of God's temple is torn by sin and evil. We do not yet see everything under Christ's feet.

Nevertheless, God has sworn to Christ that he will put all things under his feet. We have to wait patiently in faith for the final manifestation of Christ's kingdom in our resurrection. As we see the evil of the present world, the Davidic covenant assures us that our citizenship is in Christ's heavenly kingdom. As his citizens, we serve our King in this present age by letting our good works shine as a testimony to his Lordship. Our hope is not in earthly presidents, governors, or armies, but in the heavenly Kingship of Christ. He is protecting us until the last trumpet when he comes as the King of kings and Lord of lords. Then Christ will destroy all his and our enemies, especially the last enemy, death itself. And he will raise us up to be like him and to dwell with him in the light of his face forevermore.

Truly, David saw the glory of Christ's kingship when he wrote so many thousands of years ago about his reign, "He dawns on them like the morning light, like the sun shining forth on a cloudless morning" (2 Sam. 23:4). May we rejoice in Christ our King and wait in faith for our living hope in Christ, an imperishable kingdom!

Questions for Further Reflection:

1. What are the two prongs of the Davidic covenant?
2. Explain how these two prongs worked together in biblical history.
3. Why is righteousness so important for the Davidic king?
4. What are the different uses of the word *house* in 2 Samuel 7? How do these different meanings come together in the work of Christ?
5. Discuss how Christ's kingship is a comfort for you in your present life.

Dawn of the New Creation:
THE NEW COVENANT

As we explained in the last chapter, Solomon's reign initially seemed to fulfill God's promises in the Davidic covenant. David's son was seated on his father's throne, had built the temple, and was ruling over Israel in a period of unprecedented peace and prosperity. Under Solomon, Israel was at the top of her game (see 1 Kings 4:20–25). The sad saga, of course, is that their good times came to an end with Solomon's fall. Although he began well, Solomon was not faithful to walk before the Lord in obedience. He turned to foreign gods and failed to fulfill the conditional element of the Davidic covenant. After Solomon's downfall and death, Israel split into two kingdoms, with Rehoboam ruling over Judah in the south and Jeroboam ruling over Israel in the north. The books of 1 and 2 Kings (along with their counterpart, 2 Chronicles) describe the dark and dismal days of these two kingdoms and their downward spiral in disobedience and idolatry. King after king walked in defiance to the Lord and led the people in flagrant violation of the Mosaic covenant.

During this period of redemptive history the Lord raised up a long line of prophets, a series of covenant attorneys sent to prosecute his lawsuit against his unfaithful people. While Judah and Israel continued down the path of apostasy, the prophets reminded them of the conditions of the Mosaic covenant (cf. Lev. 26 and Deut. 28). They warned them of imminent doom and destruction if they did not repent. Their disobedience would lead to economic and political disaster, culminating in exile from the land.

With their message of judgment, however, the prophets also brought a message of hope. They foretold of a time of renewal that would come by God's grace through the promised Messiah. Although the people had broken the Mosaic covenant, God would not forget the unconditional promises and oath he made to Abraham. The prophets saw on the horizon a new covenant in which the blessings of the Abrahamic covenant would finally be realized. By the work of the Messiah and the power of the Spirit, there would be a new humanity and new creation. It would not merely be a restoration of the Mosaic covenant but also something altogether new, like new wine that must be placed in new wineskins.

This is the context of Jeremiah's classic prophecy about the new covenant:

> Behold, the days are coming, declares the LORD, when I will make a new covenant with the house of Israel and the house of Judah, not like the covenant that I made with their fathers on the day when I took them by the hand to bring them out of the land of Egypt, my covenant that they broke, though I was their husband, declares the LORD. But this is the covenant that I will make with the house of Israel after those days, declares the LORD: I will put my law within them, and I will write it on their hearts. And I will be their God, and they shall be my people. And no longer shall each one teach his neighbor and each his brother, saying, 'Know the LORD,' for they shall all know me, from the least of them to the greatest, declares the LORD. For I will forgive their iniquity, and I will remember their sin no more (Jer. 31:31–34).

Even though the Israelites failed to fulfill the oath they made at Sinai, God promised a new covenant in which his sacred bond with his people would not be broken.

This hope of the new covenant continued even after the hammer of God's judgment fell on the Israelites. In 722 BC the Lord sent the Assyrians to conquer and carry away the northern kingdom of Israel. Their capital, Samaria, was destroyed, and the people were scattered throughout the Assyrian Empire, never to return. Then, in 586 BC, the Lord sent the Babylonians to invade and decimate the southern kingdom of Judah. They sacked Jerusalem, completely destroyed the temple, and took the people into exile, where they remained for seventy years. Upon Judah's return to the land, the remnant continued to wait for the promised Messiah who would inaugurate the new covenant.

Then, some five hundred years later, while eating the Passover meal with his disciples on the night before his crucifixion, Jesus of Nazareth made a deliberate reference to the new covenant. Taking bread and wine, he said: "This is my body, which is given for you. Do this in remembrance of me . . . This cup that is poured out for you is the new covenant in my blood" (Luke 22:19b, 20b). With the coming of Christ—the offspring of Abraham and true Israel—the new covenant and new creation had arrived.

What Is the New Covenant?

Perhaps a better way of asking that question is, "What's *new* about the new covenant?" Since the covenant of grace is the one covenant through which all believers are saved, why did God bother making a *new* covenant? There are at least six main differences between the old and new covenants that are important to understand.

First, *the new covenant is new in relation to the Mosaic covenant, but not the Abrahamic.* As we learned in chapter 5, God's unconditional covenant of grace with Abraham was not interrupted by the conditional covenant he made with Israel 430 years later (Gal. 3:16–18). In fact, the continuity between the Abrahamic and new covenants is so strong that New Testament writers call all believers—whether Jew or Gentile—the offspring of Abraham (Gal. 3:29; Heb. 2:16; cf. Rom. 4:11). Both are covenants of promise, not law. In both, God unconditionally promises to give gifts to undeserving sinners on the basis of his grace alone, because of Christ alone. Calvin's observation of this continuity is worth quoting again: "This covenant [i.e. the Abrahamic] is so much like ours [i.e. the new] in substance and reality, that the two are actually one and the same."[1] When the Bible speaks of the new covenant, then, it speaks of a covenant that is new in relationship to what it calls the *old* covenant,

---

1. *Institutes*, 2.10.2.

that is, the *Mosaic* covenant (2 Cor. 3:4-14; Heb. 8:6-13; cf. 9:1, 15). The newness of the new covenant, while highlighting its discontinuity with the Mosaic covenant, does not create discontinuity with the Abrahamic covenant.

Second, *the new covenant is mediated by Christ rather than Moses.* An important distinction between the old and new covenants is the difference in their mediators. While Christ is the Mediator of the one covenant of grace, Moses was the mediator of the old covenant at Sinai (John 1:17; Heb. 3:1-6; 8:1-6). This makes the nature of the old and new covenants different from one another. In the new covenant, belonging to God is centered on Christ rather than Sinai.

Third, *the new covenant blesses rather than curses.* The new covenant provides the believing sinner with something the old covenant was incapable of giving: righteousness and the forgiveness of sins; as Paul says, "The righteousness of God has been manifested apart from the law" (Rom. 3:21; cf. Matt. 26:27-28; 2 Cor. 3; Gal. 3-4; Heb. 8-10). As we showed in chapter 6, the old covenant was based on law and required the national obedience of Israel in order to receive blessings. Its condition was, "Do this and you will be blessed" (Deut. 28:2). The new covenant, on the other hand, is based on God's promise to save sinners. Its condition is, "Believe in the Lord Jesus Christ, and you will be saved" (Acts 16:31; cf. Rom. 10:6-13; Gal. 2:16). In his commentary on Hebrews, John Owen underlined this distinction: "The old [covenant], absolutely considered, had no promise of grace to communicate spiritual strength, or to assist us in obedience." What it promised had to do with "temporal things in the land of Canaan."[2] The law given in the old covenant had no power to produce righteousness (1 Cor. 15:56). It could only discover, condemn, and set bounds to sin. Conversely, the new covenant declares "the love, grace, and mercy of God; and therewith to give repentance, remission of sin, and life eternal."[3] Whereas the old covenant could only reinforce the curse of sin, the new covenant *reverses* it.

Fourth, *the new covenant provides an internal renewal by the Holy Spirit.* In the Old Testament, God promised a great outpouring of his Spirit on his people in the latter days. Although Israel failed to

---

2. Owen, *Works*, 22:89-90.
3. *Ibid.*, 94.

bear fruits of righteousness, God's people would be abundantly fruitful in the new covenant because of the work of the Holy Spirit. The Spirit would produce in God's people what they were incapable of producing themselves, causing them to walk in new obedience (Ezek. 36:27). With the new covenant, the Spirit brings the new creation into the present. "The New Covenant, then, coincides with the age to come," said Geerhardus Vos; "It brings the good things to come."[4]

Fifth, *the new covenant includes the nations.* The old covenant confined the covenant of grace to one particular nation, but the new covenant expanded Israel's borders to ends of the earth, making one new man between believing Jews and Gentiles (Eph. 2:14). This, of course, involves a change in the visible nature of the covenant community. As Owen noted, the kingdom of God in the old covenant was geopolitical and earthly, "consisting in empire, power, victory, wealth," but in the new covenant it is "internal, spiritual, and heavenly."[5]

Sixth, *the new covenant is permanent.* Whereas the old covenant was temporary and designed to be replaced, the new covenant is final and irreplaceable. Because it is not mediated by a mere human but by God incarnate, who continues as our priest forever, the new covenant is permanent. Recognizing this permanency, O. Palmer Robertson points out that there is no need for another covenant: "It is not only the new covenant; it is the last covenant. Because it shall bring to full fruition that which God intends in redemption, it never shall be superseded by a subsequent covenant."[6]

---

4. Geerhardus Vos, *The Teaching of the Epistle to the Hebrews* (repr. Eugene: Wipf & Stock, 1998), 194.

5. Owen, *Works*, 22:96.

6. O. Palmer Robertson, *The Christ of the Covenants* (Phillipsburg: P&R, 1980), 277.

Figure 4 shows these distinctions side-by-side:

Figure 4. The Distinction between the Old and New Covenants

	OLD COVENANT	NEW COVENANT
Parties	God and Israel	God and believers (Jew and Gentile) with their children
Time made	Mt. Sinai	Death and resurrection of Christ
Condition	National obedience	Faith in Christ, the One who was perfectly obedient
Mediator	Moses	Christ
Promise	National blessings	Justification, indwelling of the Holy Spirit, and glorified life
Nature	Temporary	Permanent

We may define the new covenant, therefore, as *God bringing forth the new creation in his people through the finished work of Christ, in fulfillment of the Abrahamic covenant.*

What Does the Bible Teach?

In one sense, the whole Bible is about the new covenant. The entire sweep of redemptive history, from God's first promise of a Savior (Gen. 3:15) and continuing through Abraham to David and finally to Christ, anticipates the new creation inaugurated by this new covenant. Several particular passages, however, are central to understanding the new covenant.

Jeremiah 31:31-34. As noted above, this is the classic Old Testament text about the new covenant. Jeremiah says that God will make a covenant that is in contrast to the old covenant he made at Sinai: "I will make a new covenant with the house of Israel and the house of Judah, not like the covenant that I made with their fathers on the day when I took them by the hand to bring them out of the land of Egypt, my covenant that they broke." Jeremiah prophesied of a time when the old covenant would pass away altogether and new and extraordinary things would happen to God's people: "But this is the covenant that I will make with the house of Israel after those days, declares the LORD: I will put my law within them, and I will write it on their hearts." This new covenant would give what the old covenant could not: inward renewal and circumcision of the heart, enabling God's people to walk in new obedience.

This new work of the Lord in his people would be so spectacular that there would be no more need for anyone in the covenant community to teach his neighbor or brother, saying, "Know the Lord," for all of God's people shall know God perfectly, from the least of them to the greatest of them. There would be no more remembrance of Israel's sin and their violations of the Sinai covenant. Rather, Israel would walk in the perfect peace of knowing that all her iniquities had been forgiven.

Ultimately, Jeremiah was prophesying of the age to come, an age in which these things will be realized in the fullest. In the new heavens and new earth, there will be no more sin in the heart or in the mind, no more failure to know the Lord, no more discouragement over one's own iniquity. In that day, God will wipe away all tears from the eyes of his people. The former things will have passed away, and God's great promise echoed through the ages will finally come to pass: "He will dwell with them, and they will be his people, and God himself will be with them as their God" (Rev. 21:3b).

The good news for us now, however, is that this age to come has broken into this present evil age through the life, death, and resurrection of Jesus Christ. With the finished work of Christ, God's new covenant with his people has been inaugurated, and his new creation has dawned (2 Cor. 5:17). Also noted above was Jesus' reference to the new covenant on the night before he went to the cross. He referred to his atoning death, and consequently the sign and seal of his death, the Lord's Supper, as "the new covenant in my blood" (Luke 22:20; cf. 1 Cor. 11:25; Matt. 26:28; Mark 14:24). Christ deliberately used the language of Jeremiah 31 and applied it to himself.

Having ascended into heaven after his resurrection, Christ sent the promised Spirit (Acts 2) so that the blessings of which Jeremiah foretold are already being experienced in this age. Believers in the new covenant have been circumcised in the heart. God's law is not merely imposed on them externally, as in the old covenant, but internalized by the Spirit so that believers become willing to live in obedience to it.

Ezekiel. In several places throughout his book, Ezekiel foretells of the same new covenant as Jeremiah. Although he does not use the phrase "new covenant" as Jeremiah does, he uses all the same concepts, forming a clear parallel to Jeremiah's prophecy. In Ezekiel 16:60, the prophet says that the Lord will make an everlasting covenant with his people in the future. Although Israel had "despised the oath in breaking the covenant" (v. 59), that is, the old covenant at Sinai, the Lord would remember his promise made earlier in the Abrahamic covenant, "my covenant with you in the days of your youth" (v. 60), and would establish a new and everlasting covenant. Not only would this covenant be permanent, as Jeremiah also said, but it would also provide atonement for all the sins of God's people (v. 63). This covenant of which Ezekiel spoke is clearly the new covenant established by Christ, whose blood atones for our sins.

Ezekiel also said that this new covenant would bring peace to God's people—peace that comes from knowing they belong to the Lord. In chapter 34, after prophesying against the false shepherds of Israel, he reveals that the Lord will provide the one true Shepherd for his people: "my servant David, and he shall feed them: he shall feed them and be their shepherd. And I the LORD, will be their God, and my servant David shall be prince among them" (vv. 23b–24a). God would also make "a covenant of peace" with his people when this Shepherd arrived (vv. 25–31). According to Ezekiel, the new Shepherd would bring a new covenant and a new peace. This one true Shepherd, of course, is Christ (John 10:1–30), through whom we have peace with God (Rom. 5:1) and enjoy a peace that surpasses all understanding, which guards our hearts and minds in this life (Phil. 4:7).

Ezekiel goes on to speak of the new work of the Spirit in the hearts of God's people. Using language similar to Jeremiah's, Ezekiel says that God will give his people a new heart and new spirit: "I will remove the heart of stone from your flesh and give you a heart of flesh. And I will put my Spirit within you, and cause you to walk in my statutes and be careful to obey my rules" (Ezek. 36:26–27). While the Spirit was indeed active during the period of the Old Testament, creating faith (Gal. 3:7–9) and enabling believers for service (Num. 11:17; 1 Sam. 10:6), he would be poured out on God's people in a way far greater—both quantitatively and qualitatively—than anything previous. The Word brought by the Spirit in the new covenant would be such a marvelous manifestation of new life that the Lord described it as skeletons in a valley of death receiving new bodies of flesh and blood and living in joy (Ezek. 37:1–14). The new and everlasting covenant of peace would *cause* God's people to walk in new obedience (vv. 24–28).

This forms part of the background of Paul's teaching in the New Testament about the believer's sanctification. God has not only justified believers by clothing them in Christ's righteousness but he has also buried them with Christ and raised them up to walk in newness of life (Rom. 6:1–4). By the power of the Spirit, those who are united with Christ are no longer under the dominion and slavery of sin (Rom. 6:5–14), but have been freed in order to walk in paths of righteousness (Rom. 6:15–23). The Spirit is producing the fruit of righteousness in his people (Gal. 5:22–23). He also assures them that Christ has fulfilled the demands of the law for them (Rom. 8:1–4), and that they belong to God as his people and beloved children (Rom. 8:9–17). Indeed, God's ancient promises about the work of the Spirit in the new covenant are now being realized.

2 Corinthians 3. In this chapter, Paul makes explicit reference to the new covenant and shows its vital connection to the transformative work of the Holy Spirit in the believer's heart. He does this first by drawing attention to the discontinuity between the old and new covenants. He associates the old covenant with "the letter," that is, the Mosaic Law, which "kills." The new covenant, on the other hand, he associates with "the Spirit" who "gives life" (2 Cor. 3:6). Although the old covenant revealed God's righteousness in his holy law, it could not provide that righteousness to the sinner. This is why Paul calls the old covenant "the ministry of death" (3:7) and "the ministry of condemnation" (3:9). It required an obedience that no sinner could achieve, and then condemned those who failed to achieve it (cf. Gal. 3:10–12). Indeed, in one sense "the law of Moses was," as Charles Hodge put it, "a re-enactment of the covenant of works."[7]

This was to show us our need for Christ, the One who fulfilled all the demands of the old covenant. Whereas the covenant mediated by Moses was a ministry of condemnation, the covenant mediated by Christ is "the ministry of righteousness" (3:9). Through faith in Christ, and not by works of the law, we are counted as righteous in God's sight. The Spirit has removed the veil of unbelief from our minds—something the old covenant had no power to do—and is now transforming us into the image of Christ (3:12–18).

Moreover, Paul underscores the fact that the old covenant was temporary but the new covenant is permanent. In fact, the promises in the Abrahamic covenant demanded that the old covenant would pass away. Though the giving of the law at Sinai caused Moses' face to radiate with glory, the old covenant was not built to last. God designed it as a provisional covenant for his Son to fulfill. It cannot compare to the new covenant, which is permanent and far surpasses it in glory (3:11).

Galatians 3–4. Writing to churches that had come under the influence of false teachers claiming that righteousness and salvation came through works of the law rather than faith in Christ alone, Paul argues for the doctrine of justification by faith. As part of his argument, the apostle draws attention to the distinction between the Abrahamic and Mosaic covenants. The former was a covenant of promise, whereas the latter was a covenant of law. All those who desire to be justified by God must be justified the same way father Abraham was, namely, through faith alone in God's promise alone. "Those who are of faith are blessed along with Abraham, the man of faith" (Gal. 3:9). On the other hand, "All who rely on works of the law," that is, all those who try to come to God through the Mosaic rather than the Abrahamic covenant, "are under a curse; for it is written, 'Cursed be everyone who does not abide by all things written in the Book of the Law, and do them'" (3:10; cf. Deut. 27:26).

---

7. Charles Hodge, *1 & 2 Corinthians* (1859, Edinburgh: Banner of Truth, repr. 1978), 433.

Paul shows the antithetical nature of the two covenants, the Abrahamic being of faith and the Mosaic being of law: "Now it is evident that no one is justified before God by the law, for 'The righteous shall live by faith.' But the law is not of faith, rather 'The one who does them shall live by them'" (3:11–12).

Contrary to dispensationalism, however, the Abrahamic covenant did not end with the inauguration of the Mosaic covenant: "This is what I mean: the law, which came 430 years afterward, does not annul a covenant previously ratified by God, so as to make the promise void" (3:17). Rather, the promise was fulfilled in the offspring of Abraham, whom Paul identifies as Christ (3:16). All those who are in Christ by faith alone are also called Abraham's offspring (3:29). Thus, the new covenant is the fulfillment of the Abrahamic covenant. There are not two peoples of God, Israel and the church. Rather, God has only one people: the offspring of Abraham, that is, all believers of God's promise in Christ. God's promise to Abraham that he would be a blessing to the nations has been fulfilled, for Israel's boundaries have been expanded to include the nations.

But if there is such tight continuity between the Abrahamic and new covenants, it leads us to ask, "Why then the law?" Why did God bother making his covenant at Mount Sinai if it was only temporary and did not annul the Abrahamic covenant? Paul anticipates this question and answers, "It was added because of transgressions, until the offspring [read: Christ] should come to whom the promise had been made" (3:19a). The Mosaic Law was like a babysitter for Israel, "a guardian until Christ came, in order that we might be justified by faith" (3:24). It was only temporary, in order to drive God's people to Christ. "But now that faith has come, we are no longer under a guardian" (3:25).

Hebrews. The book of Hebrews contains some of the clearest teaching on the new covenant. Writing to Jewish Christians who were under persecution and tempted to depart the faith by returning to Judaism, the author of this magnificent sermon-letter argues that Christ is the fulfillment of all the types and shadows of the old covenant and the true high priest who has secured an eternal redemption through his blood. This means that "Jesus [is] the guarantor of a better covenant" (Heb. 7:22), that is, better than the old covenant mediated by Moses, for "it is enacted on better promises" (8:6). Whereas the old covenant promised blessing to the nation if they obeyed, the new covenant promises forgiveness of sins and eternal life to all who believe on the Lord Jesus.

The writer quotes Jeremiah 31:31–34 to show that God's ancient promise of a new covenant had come to pass in Christ. Returning to the old covenant, therefore, was impossible, since the inauguration of the new covenant made it obsolete. "And what is becoming obsolete and growing old is ready to vanish away" (Heb. 8:13). The sacrificial system to which his Jewish readers were tempted to return was only put in place to prepare God's people for the one true sacrifice made by "the mediator of a new covenant" (9:15). It was only "a shadow of the good things to come" and not "the true form of these realities" (10:1). It could never make sinners perfect or take away their sin. In fact, it could only *remind* them of their sin every time they offered another sacrifice.

By contrast, the covenant mediated by Christ is better because his sacrifice takes away sin and makes sinners acceptable in God's sight. His finished work ushers all believers into the Holy of Holies, behind the veil that separated the glory of God from the people (9:15–28). Thus, to depart from the new covenant in exchange for the old was to bring a curse upon oneself. "Just as the blessings of being in Christ are greater than being in Moses, the curses are greater for those who still place their faith in the shadows of the law rather than in the promises of the gospel."[8]

Why Is This Doctrine Important for the Christian Life?

The doctrine of the new covenant is important for daily Christian living for several reasons. First, *it protects us from trying to live by the old covenant*. Because we were hardwired in creation for the purpose of living righteous lives by loving God and neighbor, our natural tendency is to turn to the law to find power for pursuing righteousness. So, for example, if a Christian is grieved by the fact that he struggles with anger and impatience towards others, he might resolve to try harder at being kind and tenderhearted towards his neighbor, as God commands. In other words, in order to be more righteous, he focuses

---

8. Horton, *God of Promise*, 59.

on the command rather than on Christ, who supplies us with his Spirit in order to obey his commands. The problem with this approach is that it assumes righteousness comes by the law rather than the Spirit, which is really no different from the unbeliever's approach.

The contrast between the old and new covenants, however, teaches us the essential lesson that the law *cannot* produce righteousness. It is incapable of changing the human heart. As Paul said in Galatians 3:21, "For if a law had been given that could give life, then righteousness would indeed be by the law."

Recently, Paul's point was powerfully illustrated to the present writer when his son came home from the San Diego Zoo and retold what he saw that day at the tiger exhibit. While watching a Malayan tiger through a window in its large, walled-in enclosure, he noticed a wild duck land within the confines of the tiger's domain. The duck appeared totally unaware that it had landed in a tiger's exhibit. For all the duck knew, it had found a lovely and lush part of San Diego, a wonderful place to take a rest. But the tiger's eye caught the duck's landing and was watching its every move. Oblivious to the presence of the tiger, the duck waddled over to the stream to take a drink. The tiger instinctively and quietly assumed an attack position and then bolted for the duck in a flash. Before the duck even saw the tiger coming, it was in the jaws of the powerful creature, which tore it to shreds and consumed it as a meal. Although the tiger lived within the civilized walls of the San Diego Zoo, it could not cease from doing what came naturally. The walls could restrain the tiger, at least to a certain extent, and defined its boundaries of living, but they were powerless to change the tiger's nature. They could not keep the tiger from being a tiger. Just ask the duck.

The law is similar to the walls of the tiger's exhibit. The law defines the boundaries within which we are to live, and to a certain extent it can restrain sin. But it is powerless to change our hearts. For that, we need the recreative power of the Spirit, who has been given to us in the new covenant. As members of God's redeemed people, we are not under the powerless guardian of the old covenant but rather under the power of the Spirit, who causes us to walk in newness of life and in grateful obedience to God. The new covenant tells us that the dawn of the new creation has arrived, even in our own lives that often seem so messy. The Holy Spirit has not only imputed Christ's righteousness to us in justification but he is also imparting Christ's righteousness to us in sanctification. As we pursue righteousness, therefore, laying aside "every weight, and sin which clings so closely," we must look, not to the law for strength to live in obedience, but to the mediator of the new covenant, "to Jesus, the founder and perfecter of our faith" (Heb. 12:1–2).

Second, the doctrine of the new covenant *guards us against triumphalism*. The new covenant shows us that the kingdom of God is no longer identified with any geopolitical nation on earth. This is particularly critical to grasp in American culture, where there is a tendency to confuse the kingdom of God with the United States. America, however, is not in covenant with God as a nation. It had no representative on Mount Sinai. The only nation in covenant with God is God's new global nation, that is, his new covenant church. "But you are a chosen race," says the apostle Peter, "a royal priesthood, a holy nation, a people for his own possession, that you may proclaim the excellencies of him who called you out of darkness into his marvelous light" (1 Pet 2:9). In the new covenant, the church is no longer limited to the physical descendants of Abraham but is made up of all the nations of the earth, people of every race, color, and language. While the old covenant was an era of driving the nations out of God's holy land, the new covenant is an era of believers living side by side with unbelievers in patience and love. Today is the day of salvation, not judgment. God's judgment is delayed until his return.

Third, the new covenant *causes us to commune with God in worship*. The ancient promise, "I will be your God, and you shall be my people" (Gen. 17:7; Exod. 6:7; Lev. 26:11–12; Jer. 31:33; Ezek. 34:23–24; 37:26–27), has been fulfilled in the new covenant (2 Cor. 6:16) and is enjoyed most fully in the present age as God meets with his people in corporate worship each week. Gathering for worship, we do not come "to what may be touched, a blazing fire and darkness and gloom and a tempest and the sound of a trumpet and a voice whose words made the hearers beg that no further messages be spoken to them" (Heb. 12:18–19). In other words, we do not gather as those under the old covenant. Rather, we come "to Mount Zion and to the city of the living God, the heavenly Jerusalem, and to innumerable angels in festal gathering, and to the assembly of the firstborn who are enrolled in heaven, and to God, the judge of all, and to the spirits of the righteous made perfect, and to Jesus, the mediator of a new covenant" (Heb. 12:22–24). The Holy Spirit descends to feed our souls through the means he has promised to bless: Christ's preached Word and administered sacraments.

By the proclamation of his gospel in the public assembly of his people, God reassures us of his covenant of grace, telling us what our own hearts cannot: that his Son has satisfied the demands of his law in the old covenant and redeemed us from its curse. He kills us with his law and raises us up again with his gospel. By the power of his preached Word, he refreshes our souls with the living water of Christ (John 4:14; 7:37–38), nourishes us so that we may "grow up into salvation" (1 Pet. 2:2), and causes our hearts to rejoice in his promise of glorified life (1 Pet. 1:8).

He also causes us to commune with him by feeding us with the body and blood of Christ in heaven, who secured for us a new and living way into the Holy of Holies. "The cup of blessing that we bless," says Paul, "is it not a participation in the blood of Christ? The bread that we break, is it not a participation in the body of Christ?" (1 Cor. 10:16). When we receive it in faith, as the Heidelberg Catechism says, Christ "himself feeds and nourishes my soul to everlasting life, as certainly as I receive from the hand of the minister and taste with my mouth the bread and cup of the Lord, which are given to me as certain tokens of the body and blood of Christ."[9] Just as the preached gospel is God's new covenant promise, the Lord's Supper is his new covenant meal. Truly, we are assured of his promise and pledge that we are his people and he is our God.

Above all, however, the doctrine of the new covenant *assures us that Christ has satisfied the demands of the law on our behalf.* More than any other covenant in Scripture, the new covenant highlights the good news that God pronounces sinners justified and righteous on the basis of the alien righteousness of Christ, imputed to them and received through faith alone. The fact that God abolished the old covenant and replaced it with the new gives us assurance that

---

9. Heidelberg Catechism Q.75.

we belong to God as his children and that he accepts us in Christ. Because of this, we are able to listen to the exhortation of the writer to the Hebrews and draw near to God with confidence and pursue good works in gratitude:

> Therefore, brothers, since we have confidence to enter the holy places by the blood of Jesus, by the new and living way that he opened for us through the curtain, that is, through his flesh, and since we have a great priest over the house of God, let us draw near with a true heart in full assurance of faith, with our hearts sprinkled clean from an evil conscience and our bodies washed with pure water. Let us hold fast the confession of our hope without wavering, for he who promised is faithful. And let us consider how to stir up one another to love and good works, not neglecting to meet together, as is the habit of some, but encouraging one another, and all the more as you see the Day drawing near. (Heb. 10:19–25)

Because the Mediator of the new covenant has reconciled us to God forever, we do not find God's wrath when we come to him. Rather, we have his favor. In the place of fear we have been given a living hope, for we do not relate to God on the basis of our performance but on the basis of Christ's performance.

Having been liberated from the power of sin and the bondage of the law, we can now serve the Lord in freedom by loving our neighbor in a life of good works. We can travel through the wilderness of this present evil age, led by the Spirit who fixes our eyes on our Good Shepherd. Even in the midst of our tears and pain we can lift up our voices and sing of God's sacred bond with us in Christ, which will never be broken:

> Let us love and sing and wonder, let us praise the Savior's name!
>   He has hushed the law's loud thunder, he has quenched Mount Sinai's flame: He has washed us with His blood, he has brought us nigh to God.
> Let us wonder; grace and justice join and point to mercy's store;
>   when through grace in Christ our trust is, justice smiles and asks no more: he who washed us with His blood, has secured our way to God.[10]

---

10. John Newton, "Let Us Love and Sing and Wonder" *Trinity Hymnal* (Atlanta: Great Commission Publications, 1990), 172.

Questions for Further Reflection

1. What is the difference between the old and new covenants?
2. What is the connection between the Abrahamic and new covenants?
3. What promises of God in the new covenant did the prophets reveal?
4. What does the Lord's Supper have to do with the new covenant?
5. How does the new covenant comfort us as believers?

Glossary

Abrahamic Covenant: God's covenant of grace established with Abraham and his offspring, wherein he promised the entire future of his covenantal kingdom, in both its old covenant and new covenant stages.

Active Obedience of Christ: Christ's obedient keeping of the law to fulfill it on behalf of his people.

Alien Righteousness: A righteousness of one party imputed or reckoned to another party, namely, Christ's righteousness imputed to and received by his people through faith alone.

Common Grace: God's indiscriminate blessings on all creation, believers and non-believers alike, which are non-saving. These things include sunshine, rain, family, intelligence, art, government, and food.

Covenant: A formal agreement that creates a relationship with legal aspects.

Covenant of Grace: The covenant between God and believers with their children, in which he promises salvation through faith in Christ, who merited their salvation by his obedience in the covenant of redemption.

Covenant of Redemption (or *Pactum Salutis*): The covenant established in eternity between the Father, who gives the Son to be the Redeemer of the elect and requires of him the conditions for their redemption; and the Son, who voluntarily agrees to fulfill these conditions; and the Spirit, who voluntarily applies the work of the Son to the elect.

Covenant Theology (or Federal Theology): A system of theology that interprets the Scriptures with the biblical doctrine of covenant as the organizing principle.

Covenant of Works: God's commitment to give Adam, and his posterity in him, eternal life for obedience or eternal death for disobedience.

Curse: God's just punishment due to sin.

Davidic Covenant: God's promise to David that, when his righteous son builds a house for God's name, God will grant him an eternal kingdom.

Dispensationalism: A system of theology that interprets the Bible with distinct periods (dispensations) of history as the organizing principle. God's relationship with human beings varies according to these distinct periods. While varying forms of dispensationalism exist, all forms ultimately teach a distinction between Israel and the church, and a premillennial return of Christ. Most dispensational teachers also hold to a pretribulational rapture of the church. John Nelson Darby (1800–1882), C. I. Scofield (1843–1921), and John Walvoord (1910–2002) were significant writers in the formation and development of dispensationalism.

Federal Theology: See *Covenant Theology*. The term *federal* is utilized to describe the representative (federal) headships of Adam and Christ.

Mosaic Covenant (or Sinai Covenant, old covenant): God's law covenant with Israel, wherein he graciously leads them to Christ by showing them the perfect righteousness that only Christ could fulfill to redeem sinners.

New Covenant: God bringing forth the new creation in his people through the finished work of Christ, in fulfillment of the Abrahamic covenant.

Noahic Covenant: God's covenant of common grace with the earth, despite mankind's depravity, to sustain its order until the consummation.

Old Covenant: See *Mosaic Covenant*.

***Pactum Salutis*:** See *Covenant of Redemption*.

Passive Obedience of Christ: Christ's suffering the curse of the law for the sin of his people.

Propitiation: The turning away, or judicial satisfaction, of God's holy and just wrath.

Sacrament: A visible sign and seal that God appointed to more fully declare and seal to us the promise of the gospel.

Sinai Covenant: See *Mosaic Covenant*.

Suzerainty Treaty: A treaty between a greater king (the suzerain) and a lesser king (the vassal), which required that the vassal be exclusively loyal to the suzerain, according to the terms of the treaty.

Three Forms of Unity: (includes The Belgic Confession (1561), Heidelberg Catechism (1563), and The Canons of Dordt (1618–1619). These are a summary of the Christian faith and the doctrinal standards of Reformed churches.

Type: God revealing prophetic pictures in the Old Testament of things yet to come in redemptive history, especially Christ, his people, and heaven.

Westminster Standards: (includes the Westminster Confession of Faith, Westminster Larger Catechism, and Westminster Short Catechism). These are a summary of Christian doctrine, which was produced by the Westminster Assembly in England from 1643–1648. These are the doctrinal standards for Presbyterian churches.

Scripture Index

Genesis		8:21–22	75–76
1–4	81	8:22	81
1:6–7	78	9:1–7	76, 79
1:16–18	81	9:6	80
1:26	43, 81	9:8–17	76
1:28	79, 81	9:9	76
2	46–48	9:10	77
2:8	49	9:12	77
2:8–16	33	9:13	77
2:9	49	9:15	77
2:15	49, 51, 62	9:16	77
2:17	45, 50	9:17	77
2:23	64	12	60, 90
3	42, 46–47, 49–51, 53–54, 57, 61, 71	12:1–3	89
		15	60, 87, 90, 93, 95, 109
3:1–6	61		
3:5	53	15:3	62
3:7	45	15:4	90
3:15	18, 18, 25, 58, 61f, 68, 70, 85, 95, 140	15:6	90
		15:8	91
3:15–24	60–65	15:13	92
3:17	45, 81	17	60, 95
3:17–19	81	17:6–8	95
3:20	64	17:7	66, 148
3:22	44, 51	17:7–8	87
3:23–24	62–63	17:9–14	95–96
4:15	81	21	92
4:25	62	21:22–30	15
6:5	76	21:22–34	29, 33
7:11	78	21:27	29
8:15–19	75	21:32	29
8:17	79	22:16–18	87
8:20	75	22:17	9
8:21	75–76, 81	26:1–5	92

Scripture Index / 157

26:3	19	Numbers	
26:3–4	87	1:53	52
26:24	87	3:7–10	52
28:10–17	92	11:17	143
28:13–15	87	25:12–13	52
31:44	15	35:34	112
32:12	92		
		Deuteronomy	
Exodus		1:10	92
1:7	92	1:31	117
2:24	19, 107	4	107
3:14–18	48	4:25–31	107
6:7	66, 148	4:26–27	114
6:8	19	5:2–3	106
19	109	6:4–9	98
19:3–6	108	6:10	106
19:5	106	6:25	110
20:2	48	7:14–15	112
24	109	8:7–10	112
24:4	109	9:5	106–107
24:7	109	11:13–15	112
24:7–8	106	11:13–17	110
24:8	109	11:26–28	110
24:9–11	110	15:4–5	112
28:17–20	52	20:10	20
32	116	20:10–18	112
32:7–10	115	27:26	87, 144
32:19	115	28	135
34:10	106	28:2	138
34:10–28	115	28:7	112
40:34–35	51	28:12	112
		28:15	113
Leviticus		28:68	113
11:44–45	112	29:13	106
18:5	59, 87, 105, 113, 118	30:1	114
26	135	30:1–4	115
26:11–12	66, 148	31:9–13	116
26:38–39	114	32	114
26:40–45	115	33:27–29	112

Joshua		8:10–11	51
5	116	8:20	128
9	15	9	127–130
21:43–45	92–93	9:3	128
24	115	9:4–5	128
		9:6–9	129
1 Samuel		9:7	129
10:6	143	15:3	130
13:13–14	124	15:4	130
16	143	15:11	129
16:11–13	123		
17	62	2 Kings	
20:16	15	8:19	124
		11:17–20	115
2 Samuel		17:7–23	114
3:12	15	21:11–12	129
5	124	22–23	115
7	46, 123–127, 130	23	116
7:1	125		
7:1–17	124	1 Chronicles	
7:5	125	17	123
7:6	125	17:4	125
7:7	125, 127		
7:9–11	125	2 Chronicles	
7:11	125	13:5	124
7:12	125	15:10–15	116
7:13	127	21:7	124
7:15	126		
7:16	126	Nehemiah	
23:4	131, 134	9	115
23:5	124		
		Job	
1 Kings		33:23	34
3:8	92	33:24	34
3:9	128		
4:20	92	Psalms	
4:20–25	135	2	130
4:25	128	2:6	130
5:3	127	2:6–8	32
5:6	75	2:7	130
8	115	2:7–8	34
		16	130

16:2	34	42:6	34
16:10	32, 130	49:1–8	27
16:10–11	34	49:5	34
22:30–31	32, 34	50:1	111
40:1–2	25	50:5	34
40:3–5	25	50:5–9	32, 24
40:6–8	25–26	52:1–4	34
40:7–8	34	52:12	27
49:15	32	53	27–29
51	122	53:1–11	28
60:14	34	53:5	27
83:5	29	53:6	27
86:13	32	53:8	96
89	126, 132	53:10	27, 34
89:3	124	53:11	27, 34
89:27–28	34	53:12	28
89:34–37	126	55:3	124
89:37	133		
89:49	132		

Jeremiah

1:16–18	81
3:8	11
23:5	28
31:31–34	10, 136, 140–142, 146
31:33	66, 148
33:15	28
33:20–21	78, 124, 126
34:8–18	15
34:18	92

110	26–28		
110:4	131		
110:5–6	131		
119:105	119		
132:11	124		
132:13–18	131		

Proverbs

8:22–31	34
30:1	75
31:1	75

Isaiah

4:2	28
5:1–7	110
9:6	34
11:1	28
24:5	53
42:1	34
42:1–7	32
42:1–9	27
42:4	34

Ezekiel

1:26–28	78
16:59	142
16:60	142
16:63	142
28:2	52
28:11–19	52
34	142
34:23–24	66, 142, 148
34:25–31	142
36:26–27	143

36:27	139	Mark		
37:1–14	143	14:24	141	
37:24–28	143			
37:26–27	66, 148	Luke		
		1:32–33	132	
Daniel		1:35	33, 35	
1:4–5	75	1:80	33, 35	
9:24	34	4:18	32	
		4:43	32	
Hosea		10:16	32	
2:3	111	18:18–24	103	
6:7	53–54	22:19	137	
8:9–14	114	22:20	137, 141	
11:1	117	22:29	32	
12:1	15			
		John		
Zechariah		1:17	138	
4:12–13	34	3:16	41	
6:12–13	28–29	4:14	149	
13:7	34	4:34	29	
		5:30–43	29	
Malachi		6:37–40	29	
2:14	12	7:37–38	149	
		10:1–30	142	
Matthew		10:18	29	
1:18	33, 35	12:49	30	
4:1	63	14:26	31	
4:1–11	63	14:28	34	
4:10	64	14:31	30	
5:37	12	15:10	30	
5:45	75	15:26	31	
10:40	32	16:7	31	
15:24	32	17	34	
19:14	89	17:1–5	30	
19:16–23	103	17:2	30	
21:5	132	17:6	30	
21:37	32	17:9	30	
22:41–46	131	17:10	30	
26:27–28	138	17:11	30	
26:28	141	17:24	30	
27:46	114	18:36	132	

Scripture Index / 161

19:30	30	10:6–13	59, 138
		13:4	80

Acts

1:8	99	
2	130, 142	
2:22–36	132	
2:31–32	32	
2:33–34	131	
2:38	41	
2:38–39	97	
3:14	132	
8:12	97	
13:32–39	132	
13:33	34	
14:17	75	
16:31	59, 138	

1 Corinthians

6:19	132
10:11	119
10:16	149
11:25	141
15:21–22	32, 54–55
15:25	131
15:45	55
15:56	138

Romans

1:4	34, 35
2:14–15	53, 81
3:19–20	104
3:21	117, 138
3:26	117
4	91
4:5	117
4:11	87, 96, 137
5:1	142
5:8–10	37
5:12	45
5:12–19	31–32, 54–55
5:14	54
5:19	32, 54, 59
5:19–20	54
6:1–4	143
6:5–14	143
6:15–23	143
8:1–4	143
8:3	34
8:9–17	143
8:11	33, 35
8:28–30	74

2 Corinthians

3	11, 138, 143
3:4–14	138
3:6	143
3:7	143
3:9	144
3:11	144
3:12–18	144
5:17	141
5:21	116
6:16	66, 148

Galatians

2:16	59, 138
3	19
3:6–9	87
3:7–9	93, 143
3:9	144
3:10–12	87, 144
3:11–12	87, 145
3:12	59
3:13	93, 99
3:15–22	32
3:16	87, 93, 145
3:16–18	137
3:17	94, 145
3:17–18	88
3:17–19	106

3:19	88, 145	**1 Timothy**	
3:21	147	2:5	59
3:23–26	88	4:4–5	80
3:24	104, 145	6:17	80
3:25	145		
3:28	97, 99	**2 Timothy**	
3:29	62, 87, 94–95, 99, 137, 145	1:9	31
3–4	11, 138, 144	**Hebrews**	
4:4	34, 119	1:1–13	32
5:22–23	143	2:8	133
		2:9–10	34
Ephesians		2:14–16	64
1:3–14	30–31	2:16	87, 137
1:7	31	3:1–6	138
1:8–10	31	5:5–6	32
1:11–12	31	5:7	34
1:13–14	31	5:8	32
2:1–3	45	7	26
2:8–9	68	7:17	27
2:12	97, 114	7:20–21	27
2:14	139	7:21	34
2:19	97	7:22	36, 145
2:20–22	132	7:25	34
3:8–12	32	7:28	27, 34
4:24	44	8:1–6	138
6:1	97	8:6	36, 146
6:4	98	8:6–13	138
		8:13	146
Philippians		9:1	138
2:6–7	34	9:14	33, 35
2:6–8	28, 34	9:15	36, 138, 146
2:9–11	28	9:15–28	146
4:7	142	9:24	34
		10:1	146
Colossians		10:5–9	34
2:11–12	96	10:5–10	26
4:16	98	10:19–20	99
		10:19–25	150
1 Thessalonians		11:8–10	95
5:27	98	11:9–10	113

11:13–16	95
12:1–2	148
12:2	32, 34
12:7–8	12
12:14	103
12:18–19	148
12:22–24	149
12:24	36
13:20	32

1 Peter

1:4	95
1:8	149
2	80
2:2	149
2:5	132
2:9	99, 148
3:18	35

2 Peter

3:5–7	81

Revelation

21:2–3	66
21:3	20, 133, 141
21:27	113
22:2	44

Name Index

A
Augustine, 42

B
Baugh, S. M., 36
Beale, G. K., 52n
Belgic Confession, 44, 68–69
Berkhof, Louis, 16, 38, 43
Bolton, Samuel, 105, 107

C
Calvin, John, 44, 87, 107, 137
Clowney, Edmund, 69–70
Cocceius, Johannes, 105
Curtis, Byron, 54n

G
Gillespie, Patrick, 105

H
Haran, Menahem, 15
Heidelberg Catechism, 38, 42, 44, 67–69, 88–89, 105, 149
Hodge, Charles, 144
Horton, Michael, 17, 39, 65–66, 146

K
Kline, Meredith, 29n, 61, 79, 85–86, 89n

M
Mettinger, Tryggve N. D., 48

N
Newton, John, 10n
Olevianus, Caspar, 42, 67, 105
Owen, John, 33–35, 105, 111, 138–139

P
Perkins, William, 67, 105
Petto, Samuel, 117
Polanus, Amandus, 67, 105

R
Robertson, O. Palmer, 139
Rollock, Robert, 67, 105

S
Savoy Declaration of Faith, 33
Sibbes, Richard, 105
Strong, William, 105

T
Tolkien, J. R. R., 57, 85
Turner, Laurence A., 78n
Turretin, Francis, 20, 105

U
Ursinus, Zacharias, 42, 67, 105
Ussher, James, 105

V
Vos, Geerhardus, 37, 49n, 139

W
Waltke, Bruce, 50
Warfield, B. B., 89
Webb, Barry, 48
Westminster Confession of Faith, 33, 43, 67–69, 111
Westminster Larger Catechism, 68–69
Westminster Shorter Catechism, 43, 45
Witsius, Herman, 35, 105
Wollebius, Johannes, 67, 105

Note to the Reader

The publisher invites you to respond to us about this book by writing Reformed Fellowship, Inc., 3500 Danube Dr. SW, Grandville, MI 49418-8387 USA. You may also email us at *president@reformedfellowship.net*

Founded in 1951, Reformed Fellowship is a religious and strictly nonprofit organization composed of a group of Christian believers who hold to the biblical Reformed faith. Our purpose is to advocate and propagate this faith, to nurture those who seek to live in obedience to it, to give sharpened expression to it, to stimulate the doctrinal sensitivities of those who profess it, to promote the spiritual welfare and purity of the Reformed churches, and to encourage Christian action.

Members of Reformed Fellowship express their adherence to the Calvinistic creeds as formulated in the Belgic Confession, the Heidelberg Catechism, the Canons of Dort, and the Westminster Confession and Catechisms.

To fulfill our mission, we publish a bi-monthly journal, *The Outlook*, and we publish books and Bible study guides. Our website is *www.reformedfellowship.net*